Shared Eye

Sadie Benning

The Renaissance Society

Kunsthalle Basel

Contents

Foreword

Solveig Øvstebø and Elena Filipovic

The title of Sadie Benning's exhibition *Shared Eye* evokes the idea of a shared way of seeing. Following its lead, one might reimagine vision as a collaboration between individuals, a process inextricable from its many, often conflicting, sources and participants. Perhaps fittingly, the exhibition itself was a collaboration between two institutions: The Renaissance Society and Kunsthalle Basel. It took different forms in Chicago and Basel, but in each case the exhibition was grounded by an ambitious new project, also titled *Shared Eye*, consisting of a sequence of forty panels. (Benning created the ensemble to fit perfectly in the space at the Ren and then augmented it with a selection of complementary works for the additional galleries at Kunsthalle Basel.) Each panel in *Shared Eye* is composed of large mounted digital snapshots taken with the artist's smartphone, embedded with painted aqua resin elements and smaller found photographs that are drawn from various sources, ranging from strangers' family photos to newspaper telefax images. Many of the works are punctuated by miniature toys or keepsakes presented upon tiny sculpted shelves.

Elusive connections emerge among a work's different elements. They juxtapose the intimate and the anonymous, the digital present and an indeterminate analog past, the miniature and the monumental, the extreme close-up and the aerial view. Produced in the months leading up to the US presidential election in 2016, *Shared Eye* is partially the artist's highly personal response to the state of the world at a moment of deep political uncertainty, while at the same time being generously open to the viewer's own impressions and interpretations. Each piece, the artist attests, "serves as a visual representation of the past, the present, and the future, colliding." They are imbued with the charge of what has come before and what is yet to come.

The past shadows the work in other ways, too. Benning created *Shared Eye* in response to a 1976 series of paintings by the late German artist Blinky Palermo, titled *to the people of N.Y.C.* Made shortly before Palermo died and never exhibited in his lifetime, *to the people of N.Y.C.* left an impact on Benning, who saw them on view at Dia Beacon. Palermo's installation is composed of forty nonrepresentational paintings on metal, presented in a rhythmic pattern of different sizes, proportions, and proximities, and arranged in fifteen sequences.[1] In her wonderfully insightful contribution in this book, Christine Mehring delves into both Palermo's installation and Benning's response, reflecting on the complexities of both. *Shared Eye* follows the parameters of Palermo's installation, appropriating the late artist's idiosyncratic specifications, but there is no overt relationship between the content of Benning's and Palermo's works. Instead it is a mathematical connection or a numerical ratio that quietly binds them. In so doing, Benning highlights the ways that we insert our own histories and ideas into the frames we encounter.

The works in *Shared Eye* hover between mediums, defying easy categorization, acting simultaneously as drawings, sculptures, photographic works, and even paintings. On a deeper level, they also carry forward Benning's own history, and long experience, with moving images. Throughout the 1990s, Benning created an extraordinary body of experimental video work, improvising with materials at hand and a toy camera. More than two decades later, the handmade aesthetic, grainy imagery, and durational logic explored in the earlier videos has expanded and taken on a different form in *Shared Eye*, as the artist confronts a different moment in history. When speaking of this new work, Benning persistently invokes

1
Lynne Cooke, "An-Other Alexandrian," *To the People of New York City* (New York: Dia Art Foundation and Düsseldorf: Richter Verlag GmbH, 2011), 175.

film editing techniques—cuts, pans, fades, pauses, and staccato transitions—and alludes to the logic of the film loop. In his essay for this book, John Corbett elaborates lyrically on various cinematic aspects of the work, which he describes as a "symphonic arrangement." As Corbett suggests, the experience of the ensemble is spatial and textural, but also temporal; meaning emerges not only within the still-image compositions of *Shared Eye* but also in the dialogues between them.

Lynne Cooke, the former chief curator at the Dia Foundation, describes Palermo's *to the people of N.Y.C.* as "a resonant ensemble at once vast and intimate, cohesive and fragmentary, declarative and ambivalent, limpid and obtuse."[2] One might describe *Shared Eye* the same way. Benning designed the works in *Shared Eye* to question how we experience the world, both collectively and alone, and each piece functions individually and as part of the larger group. In the illuminating conversation between Benning and Julie Ault reproduced in this volume, it becomes clear how rich and complex this multivalent project is. The two discuss Benning's working process, the surrounding political climate, the value of hybrid mediums, the work's relationship to video and music, editing and loops, improvisation, time, photography and memory, Blinky Palermo, and the nature of found images and objects, among many other things. *Shared Eye* is born of a particular artist's mind at an unsettling, and perhaps unprecedented political moment, but also transcends it in many ways. We are deeply grateful that Sadie Benning chose to create *Shared Eye* for these exhibitions at the Renaissance Society and Kunsthalle Basel. These works stay with us, leaving a layered afterimage in our minds.

2

Ibid., 179.

Shared Eye

All works of the *Shared Eye* series:

Acrylic, aqua resin, casein, digital images, found material, photographs, wood

Sequence 1: Panels 1–3

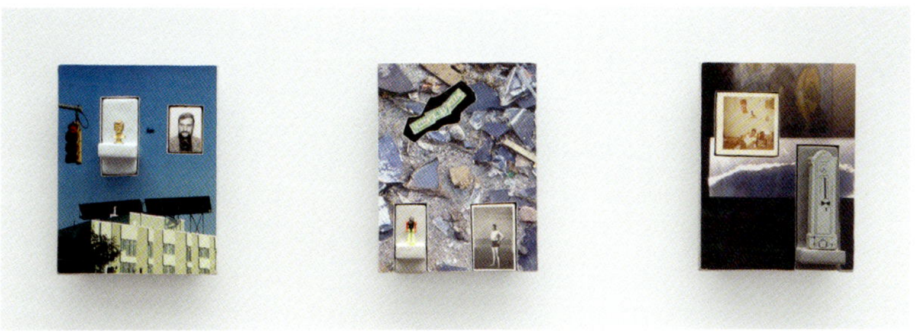

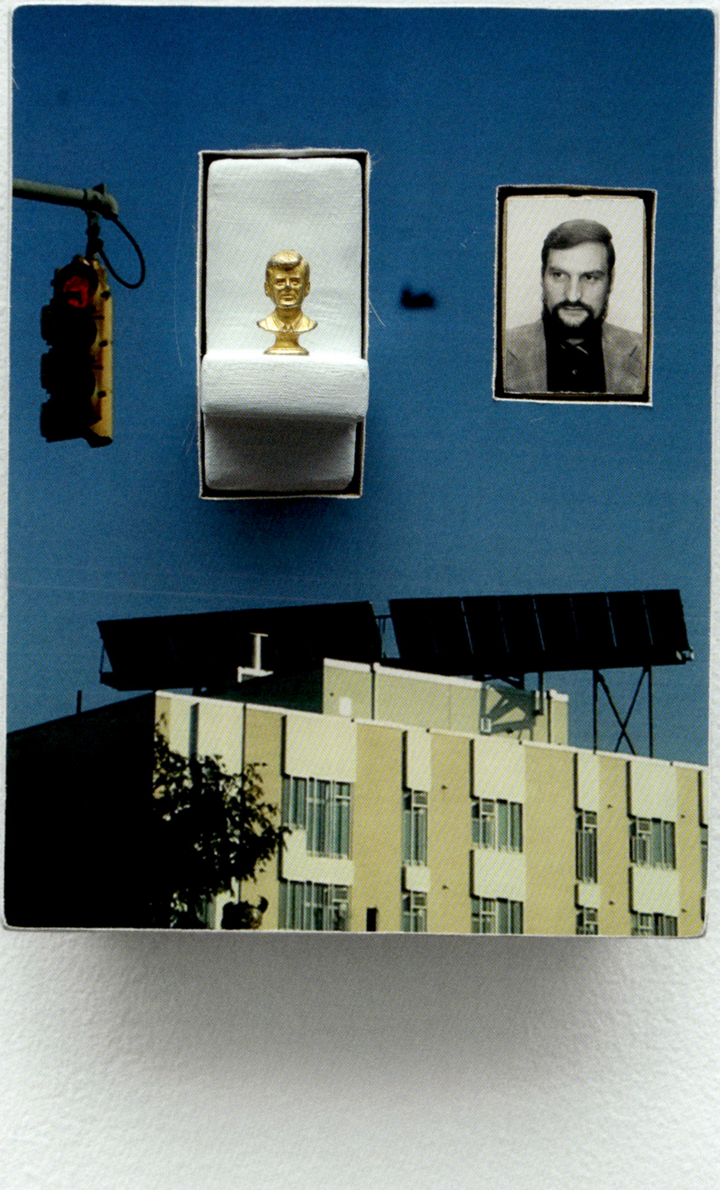

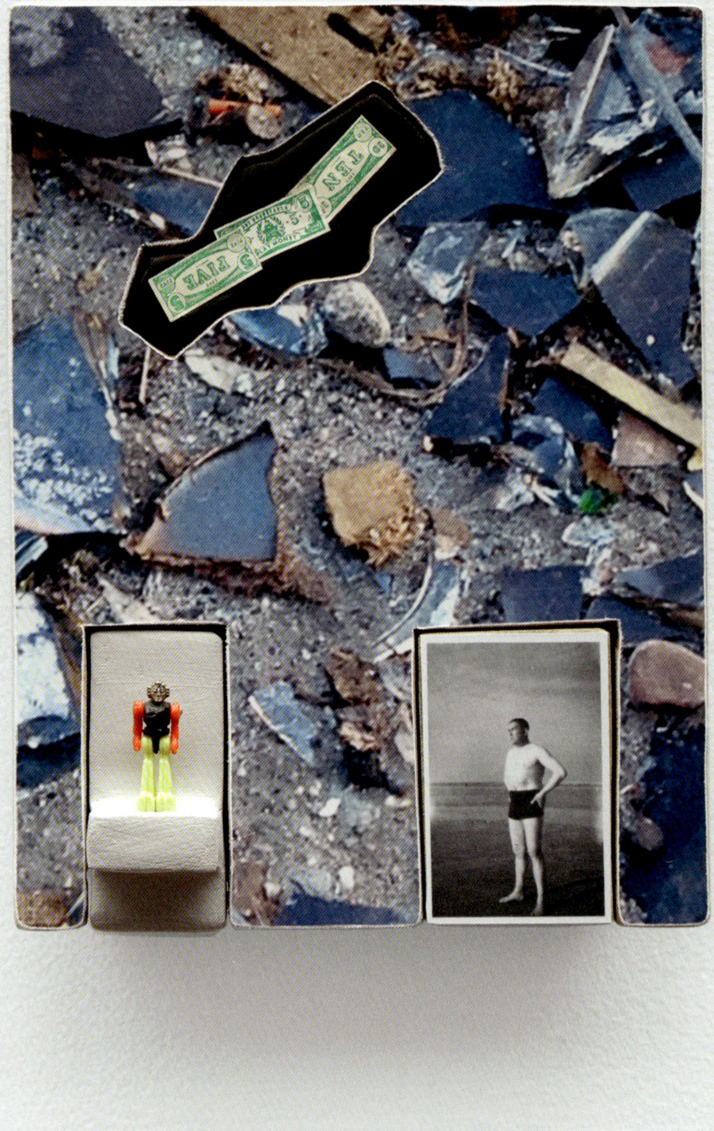
TEN
FIVE

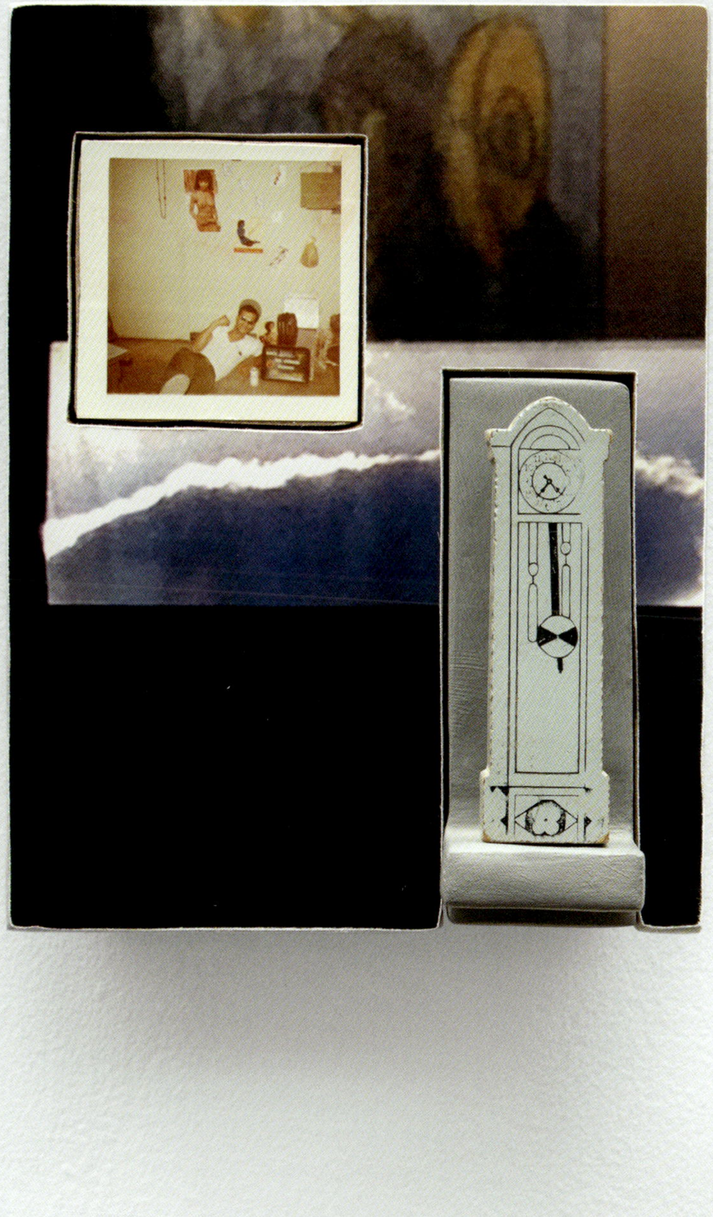

Sequence 2: Panels 4–7

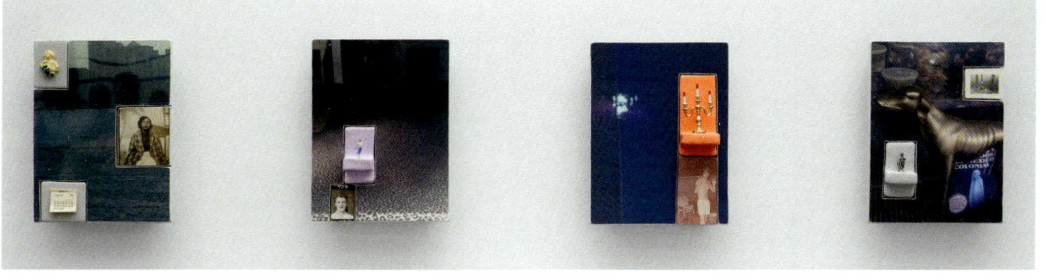

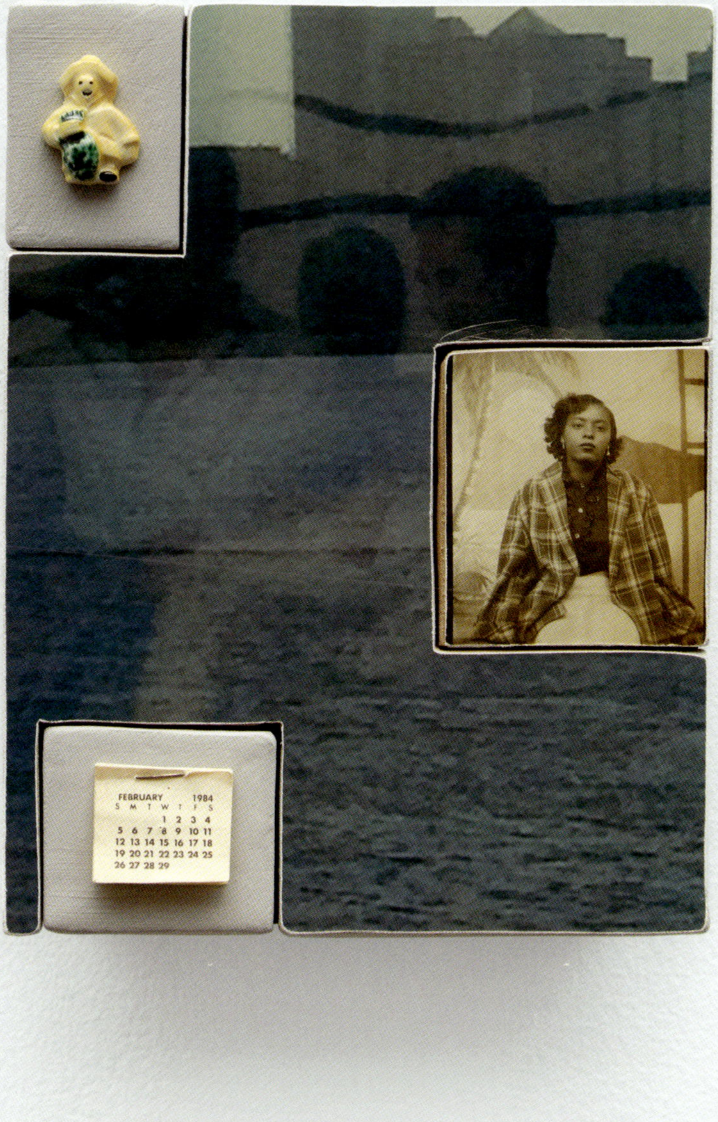
FEBRUARY 1984
S M T W T F S
1 2 3 4
5 6 7 8 9 10 11
12 13 14 15 16 17 18
19 20 21 22 23 24 25
26 27 28 29

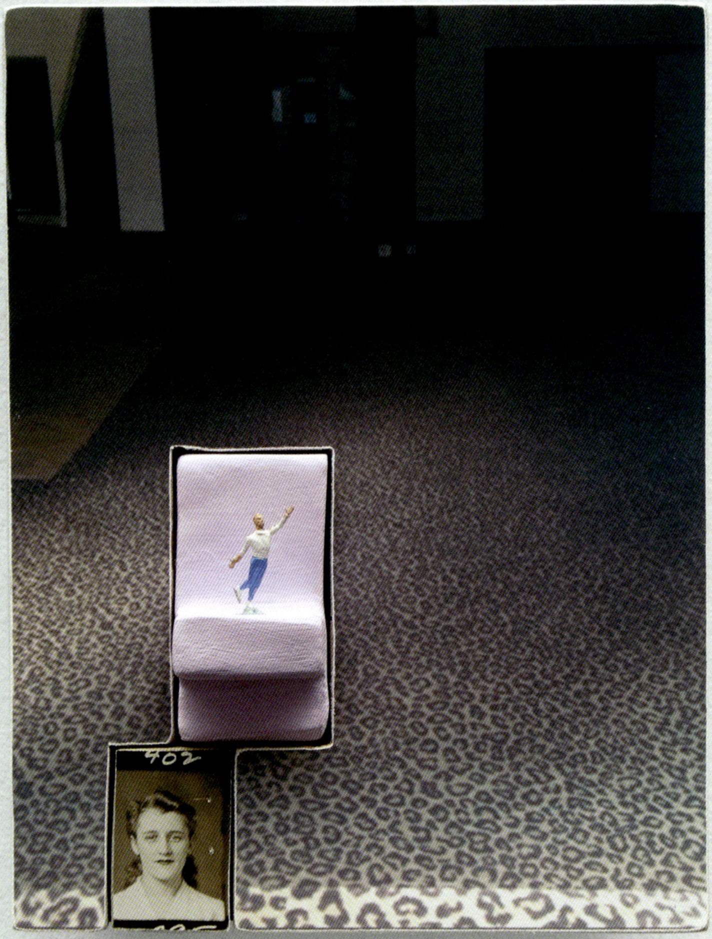

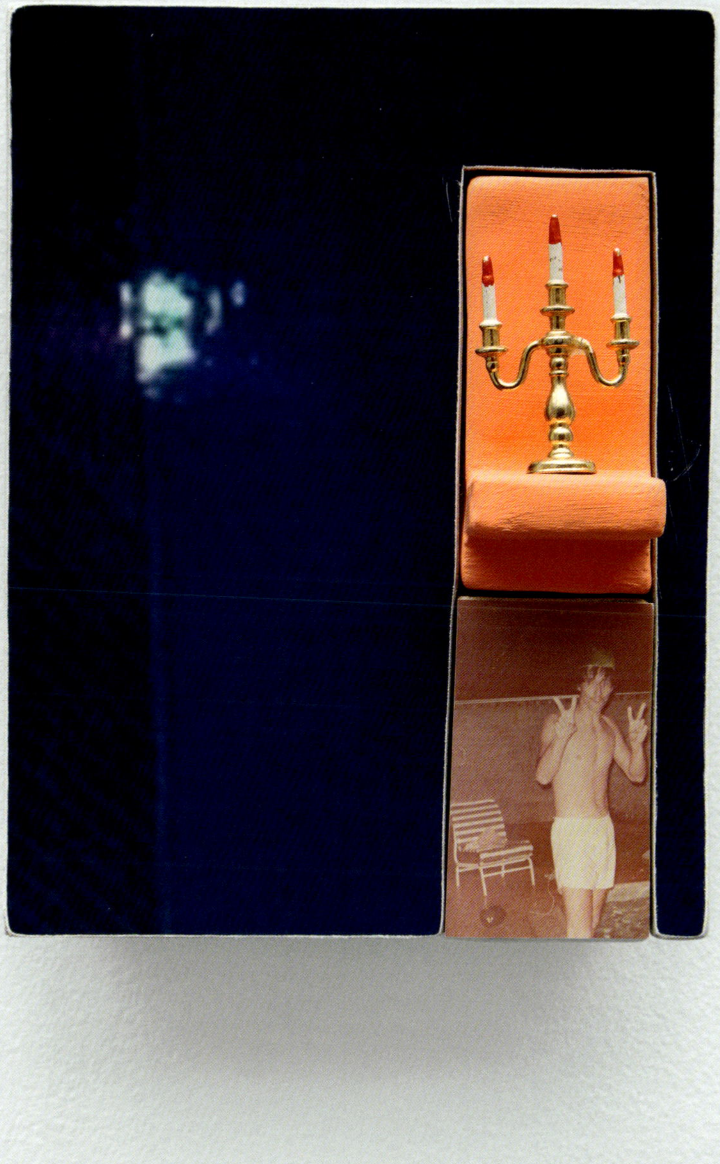

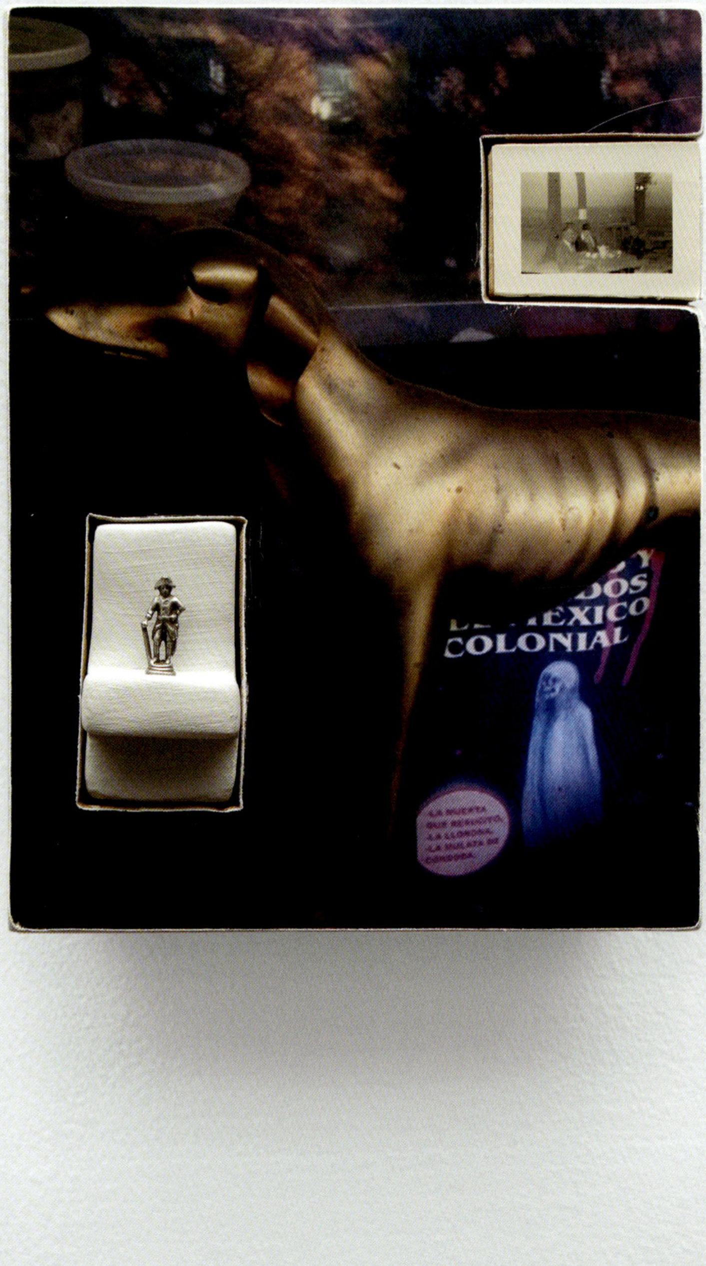
COLONIAL

Sequence 3: Panels 8–10

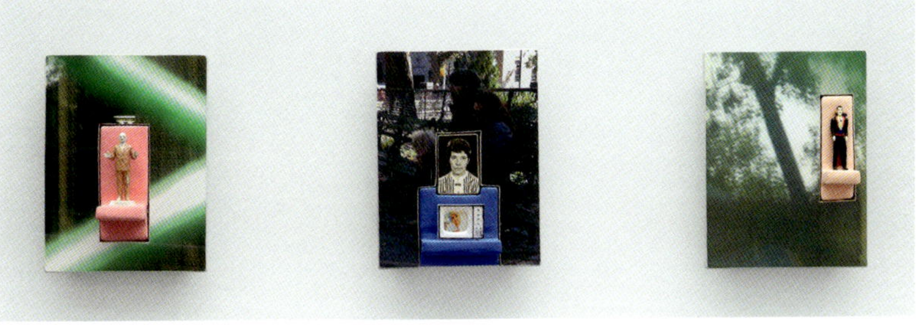

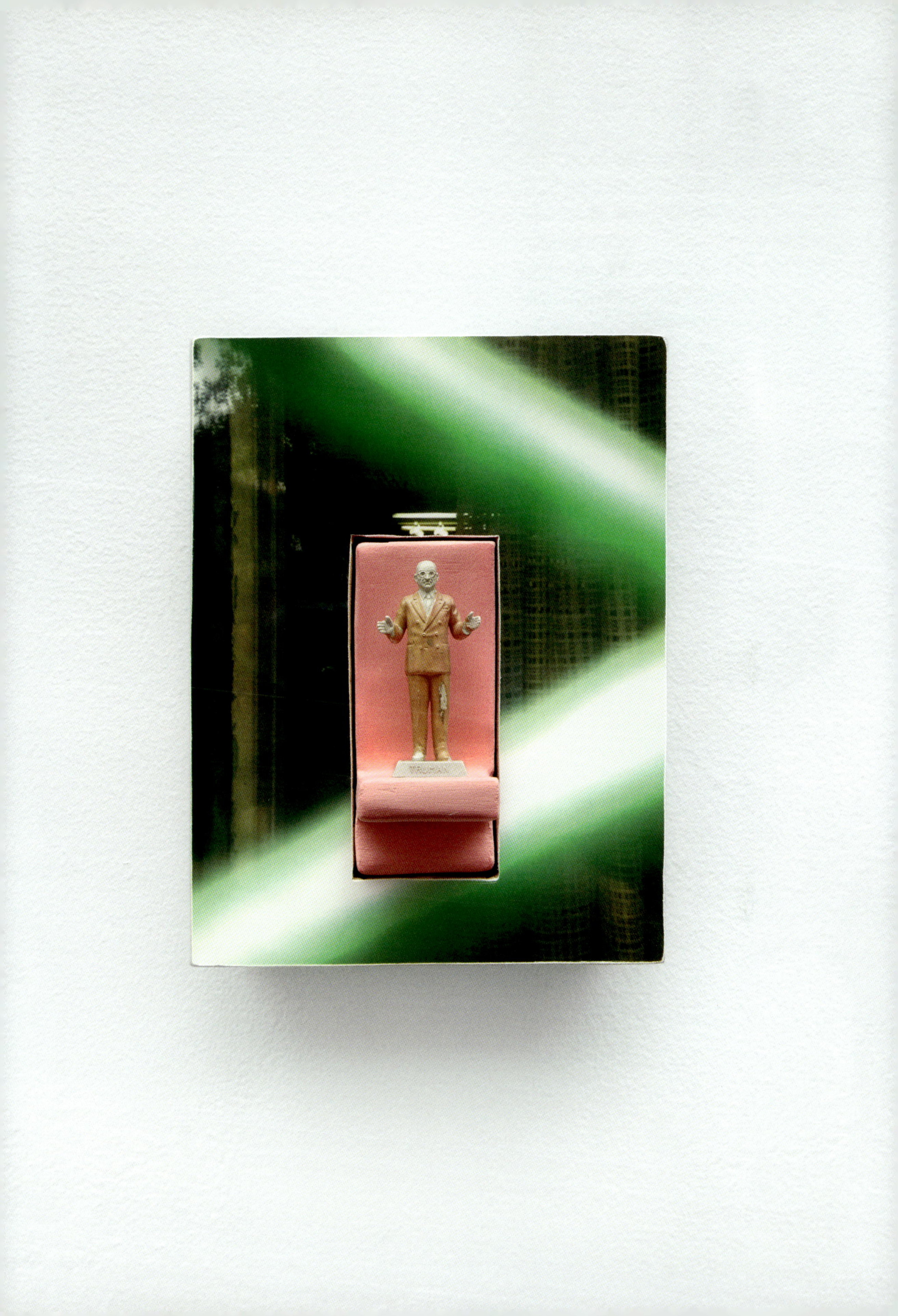

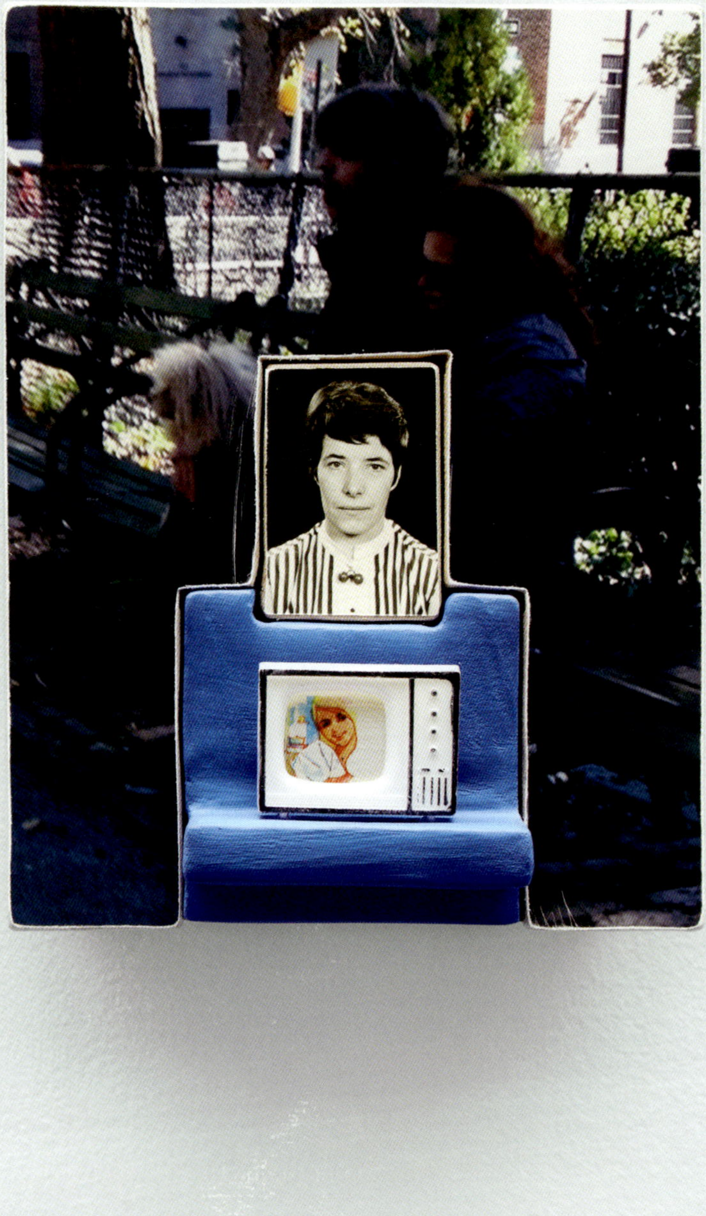

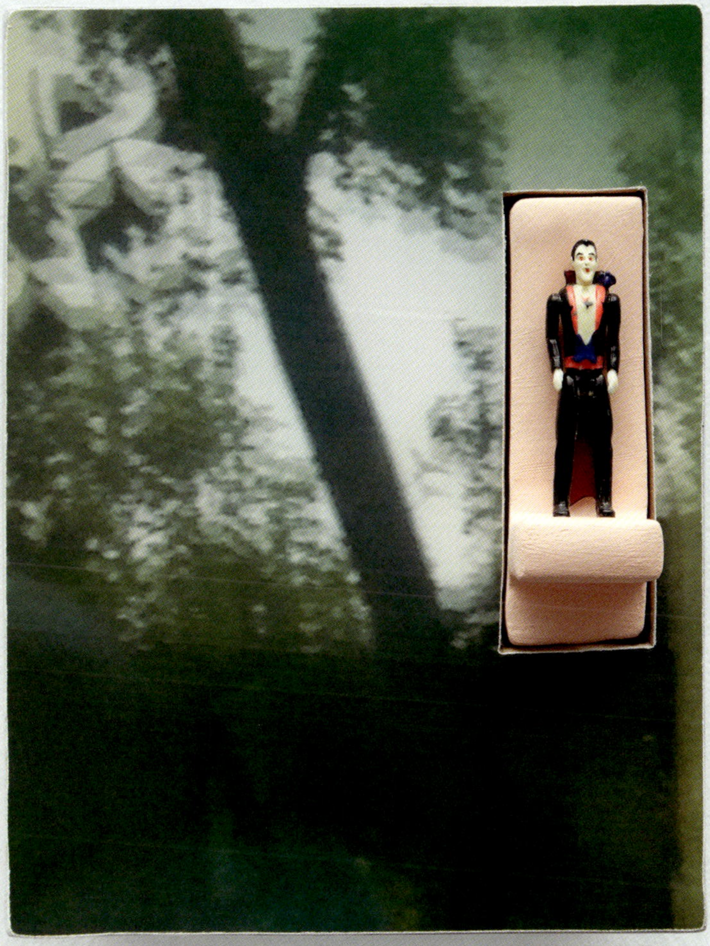

Sequence 4: Panels 11–14

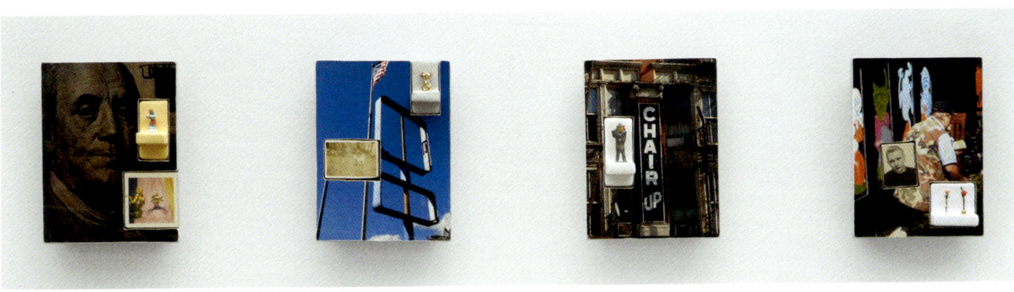
CHAIR
UP

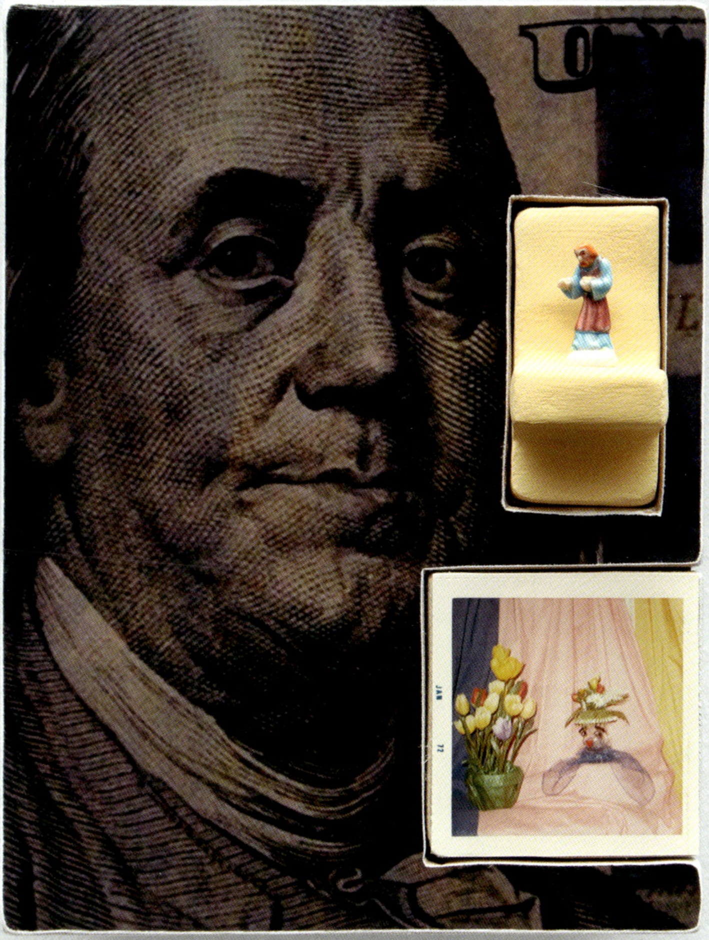

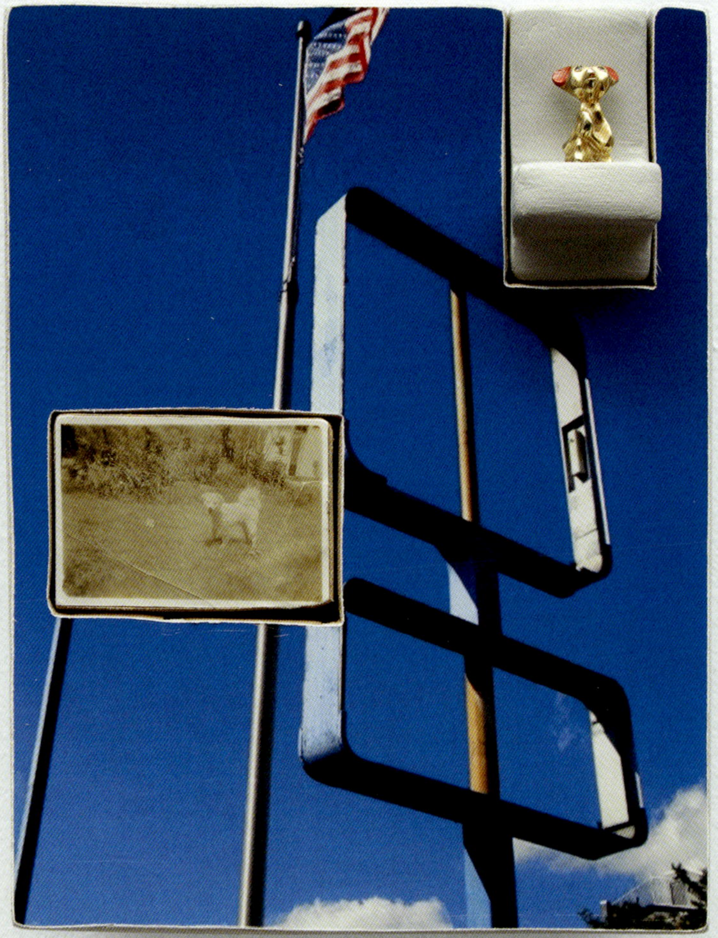

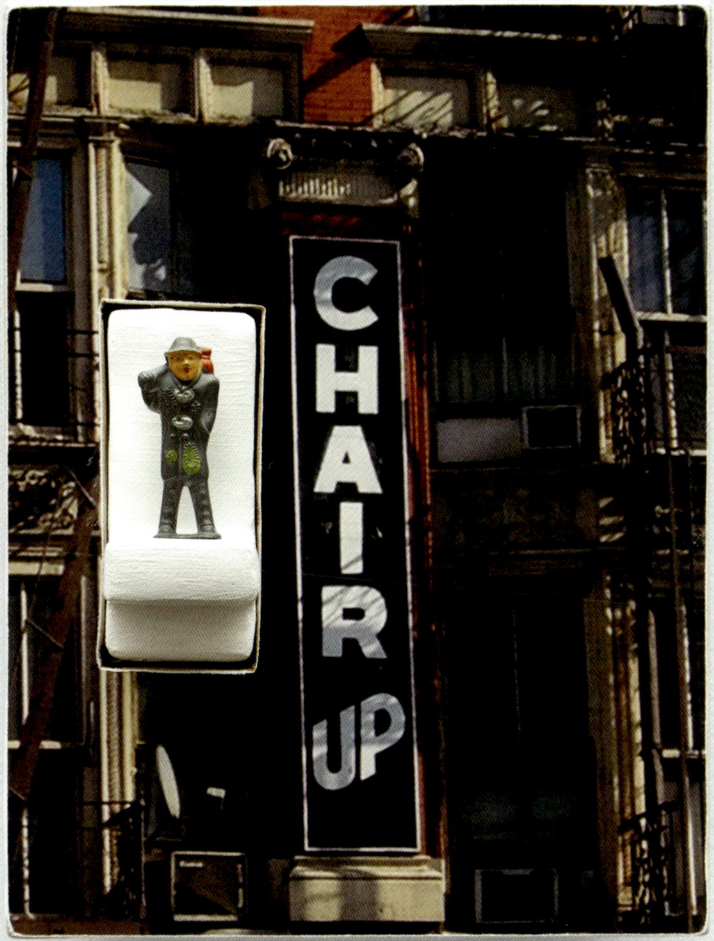
CHAIR
UP

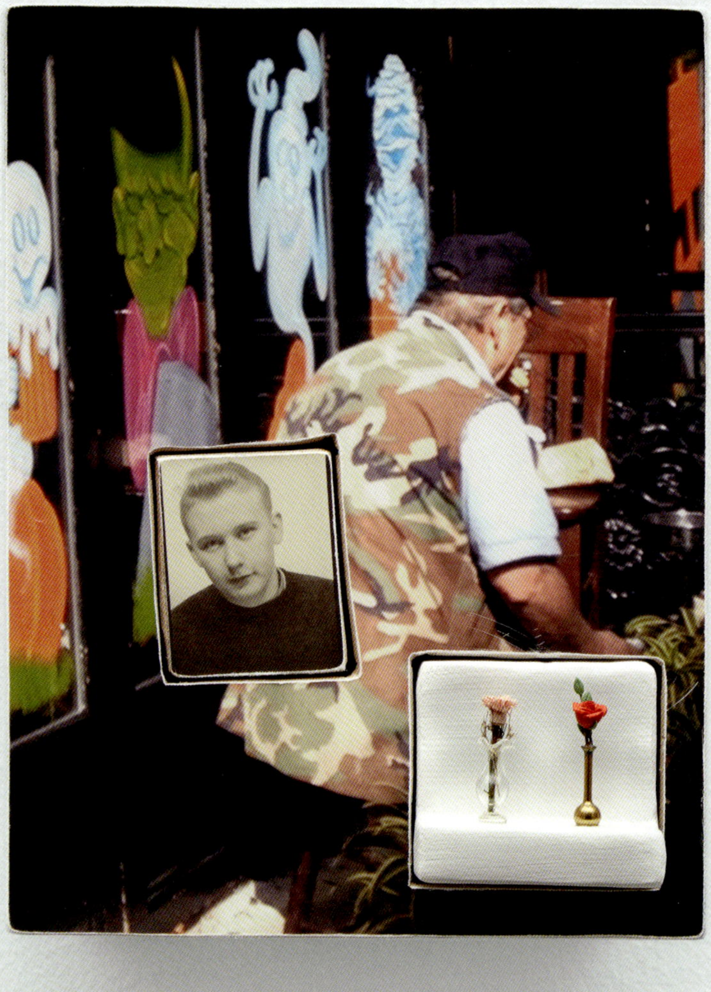

Sequence 5: Panels 15–17

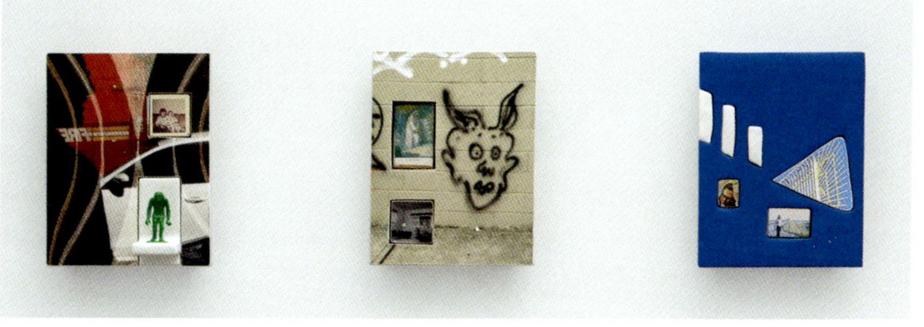

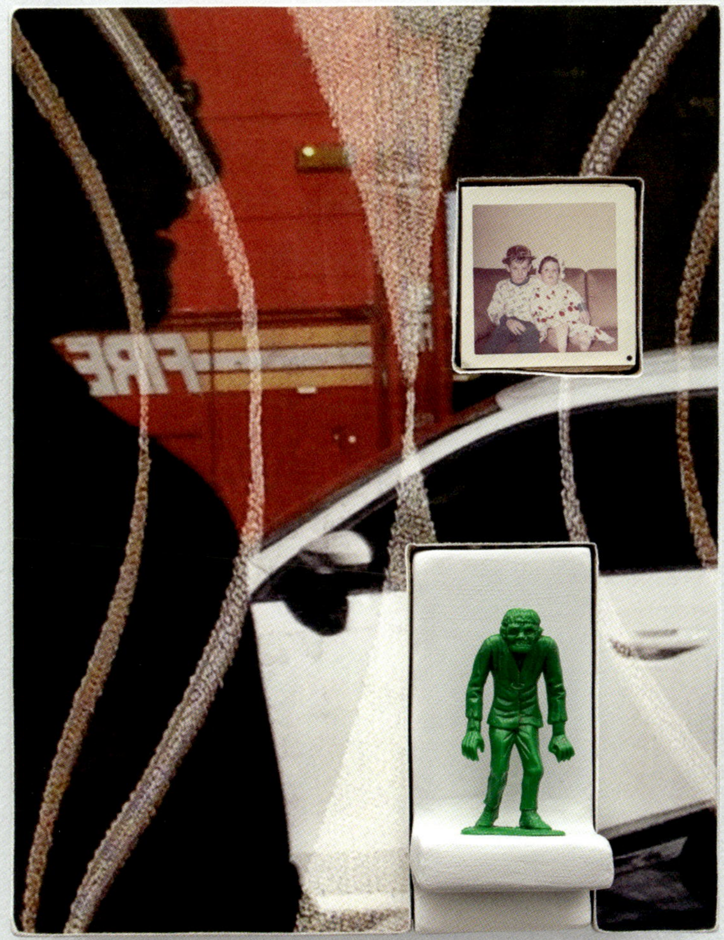

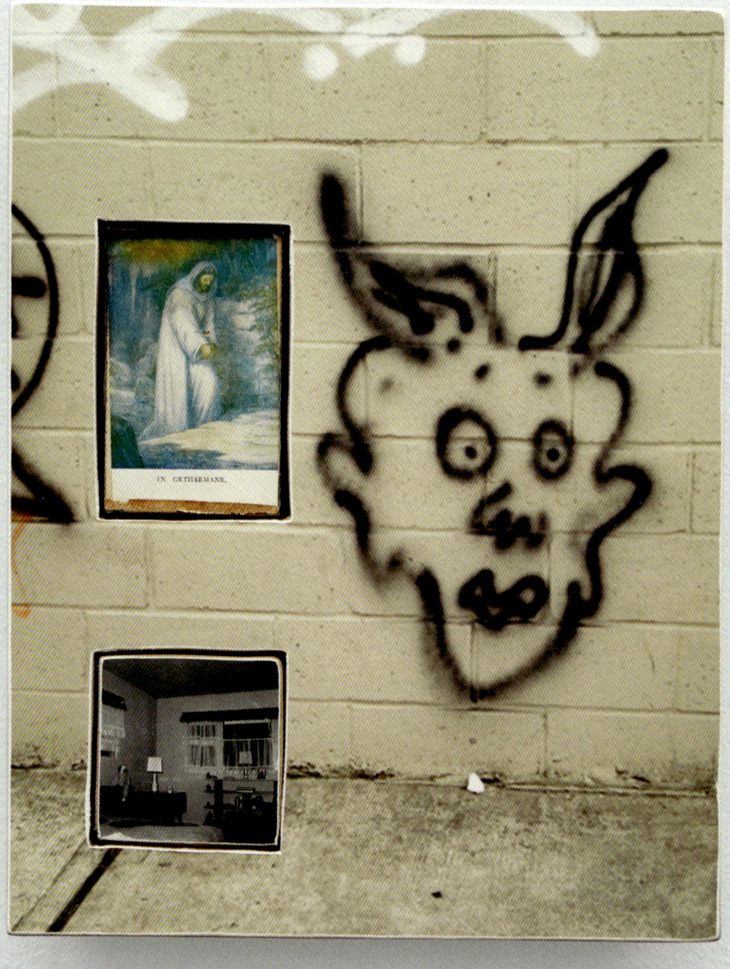
IN GETHSEMANE.

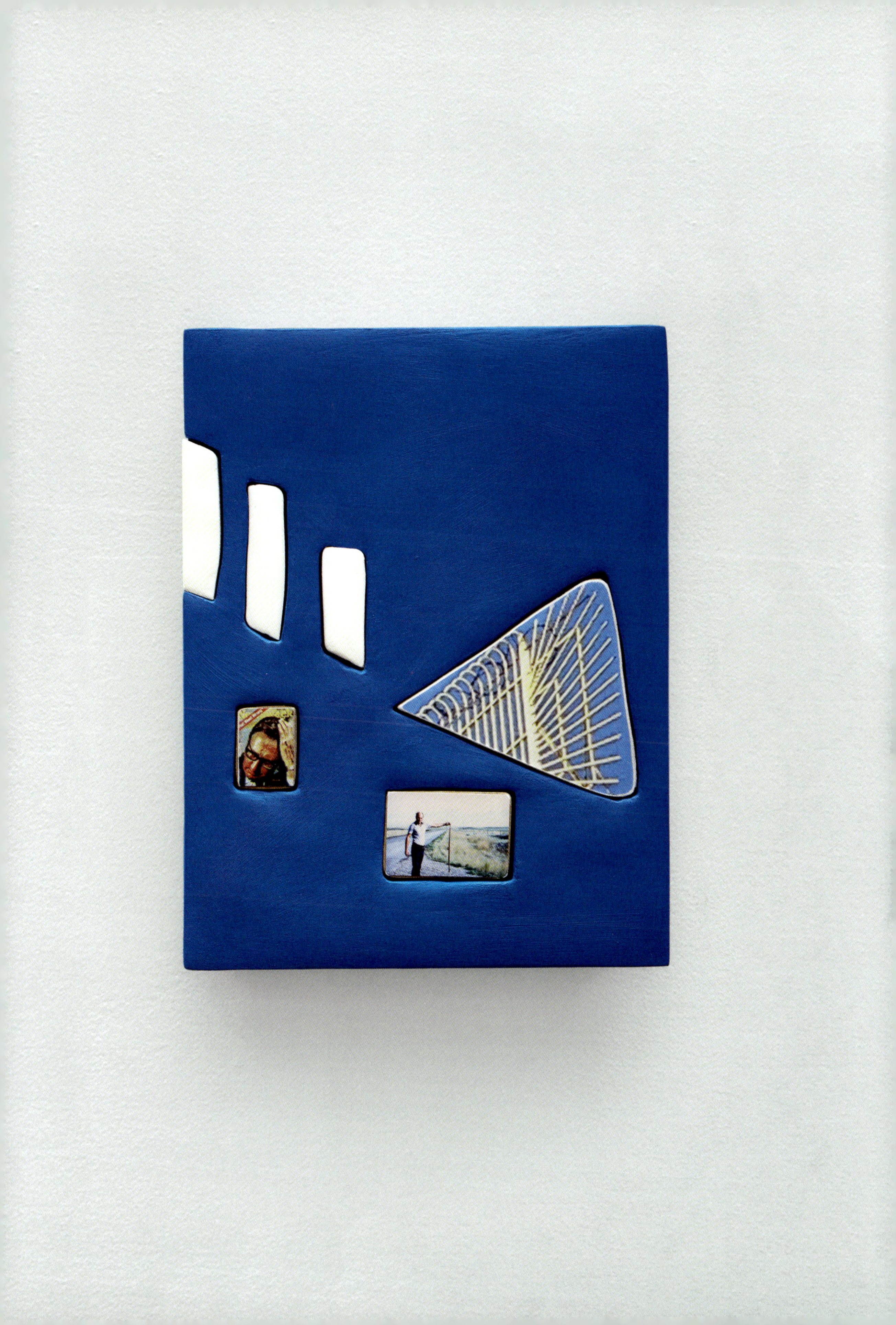

Sequence 6: Panels 18|19

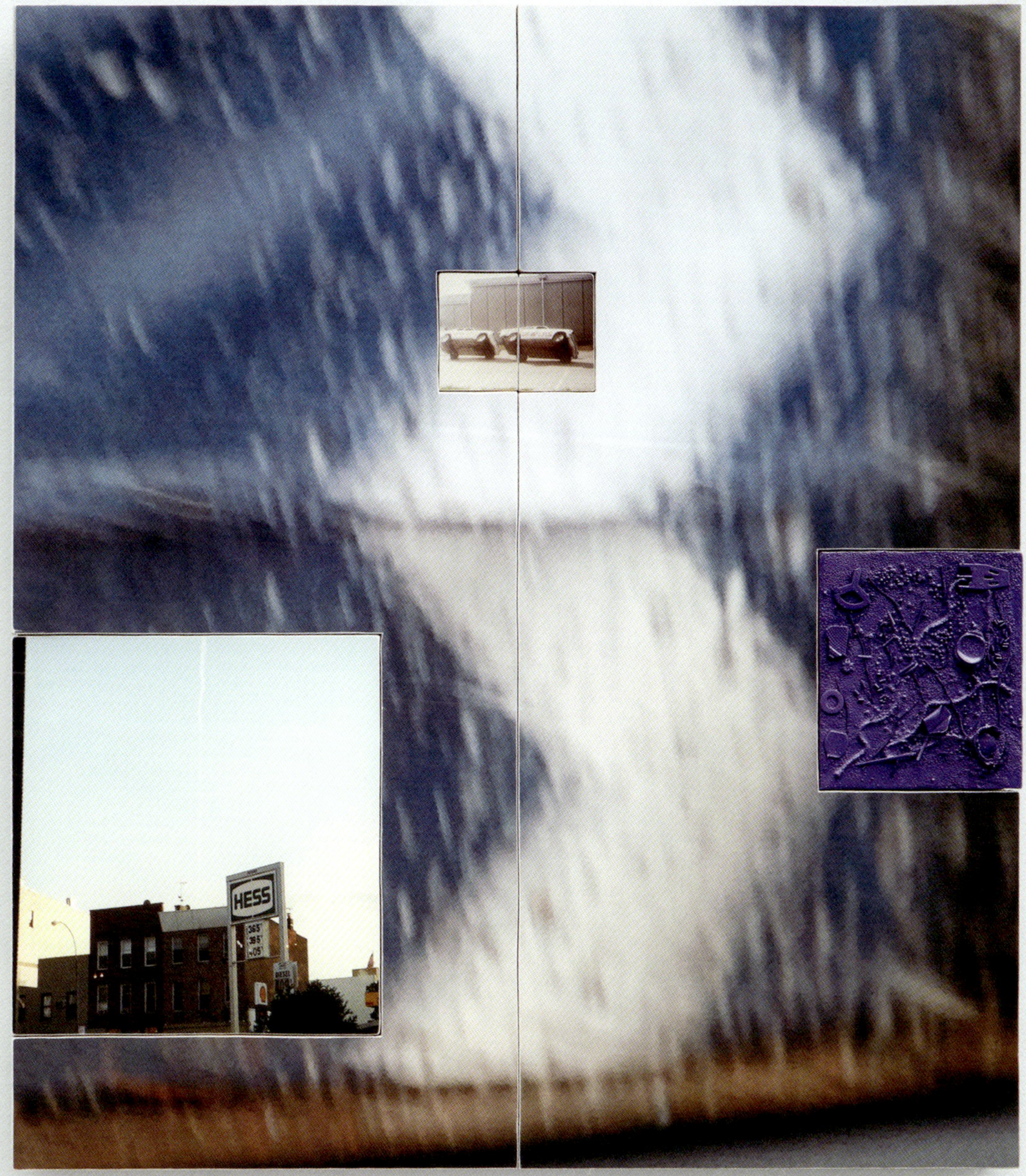
HESS

Sequence 7: Panels 20–23

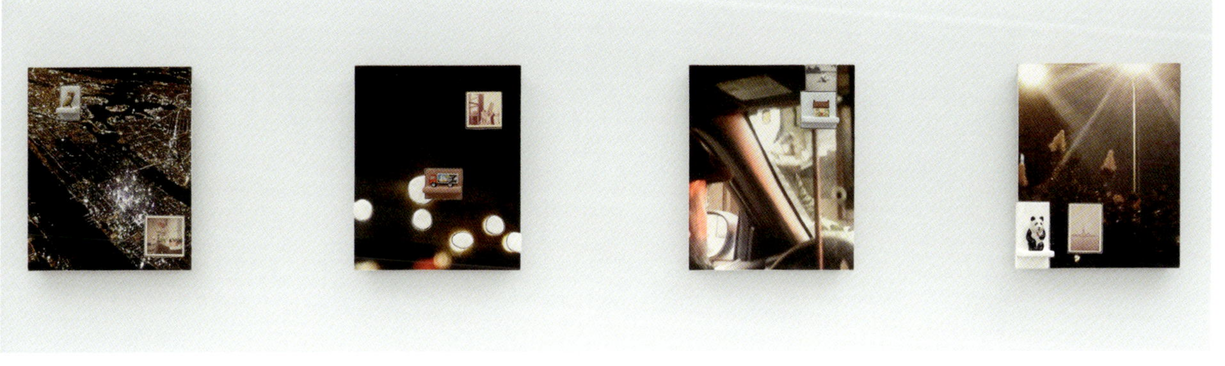

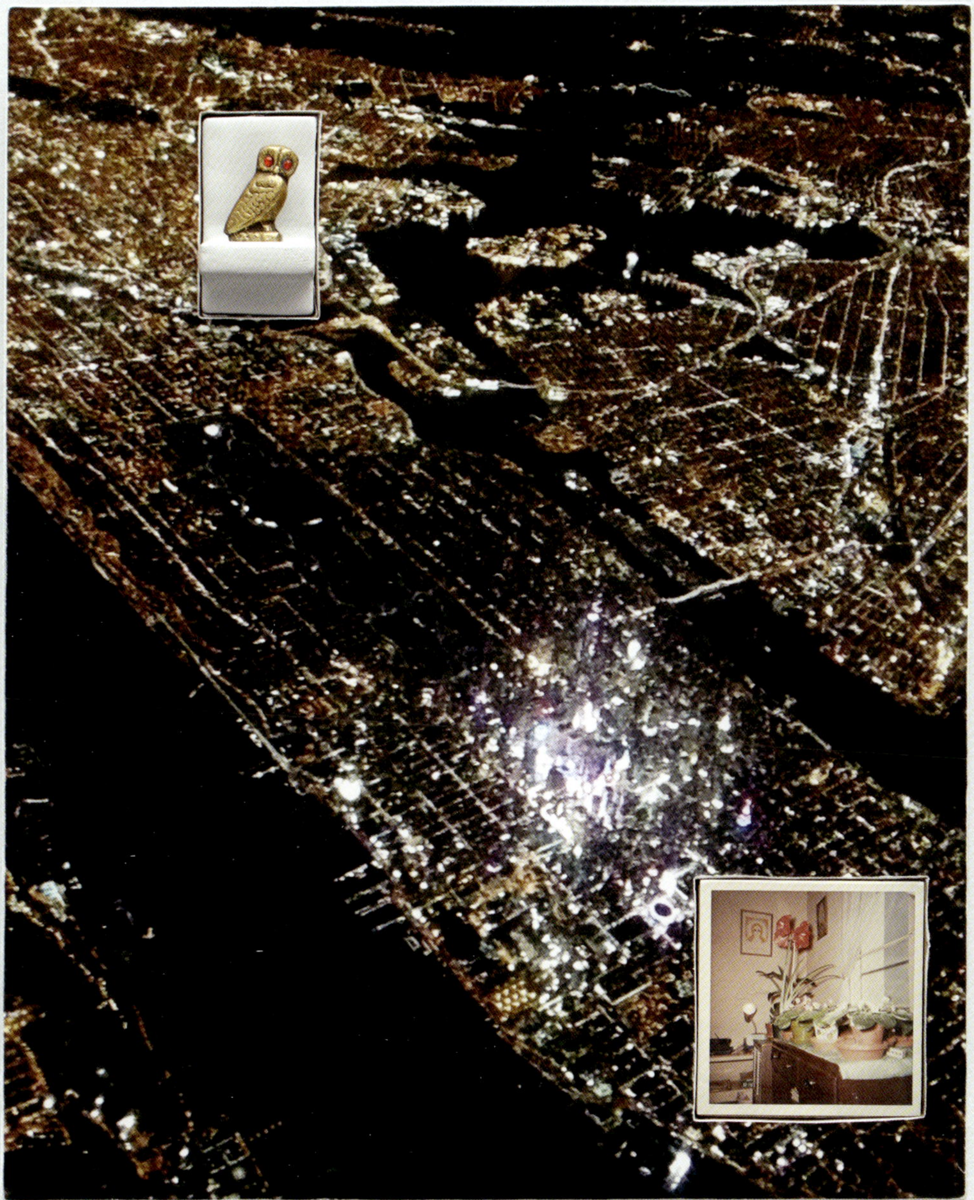

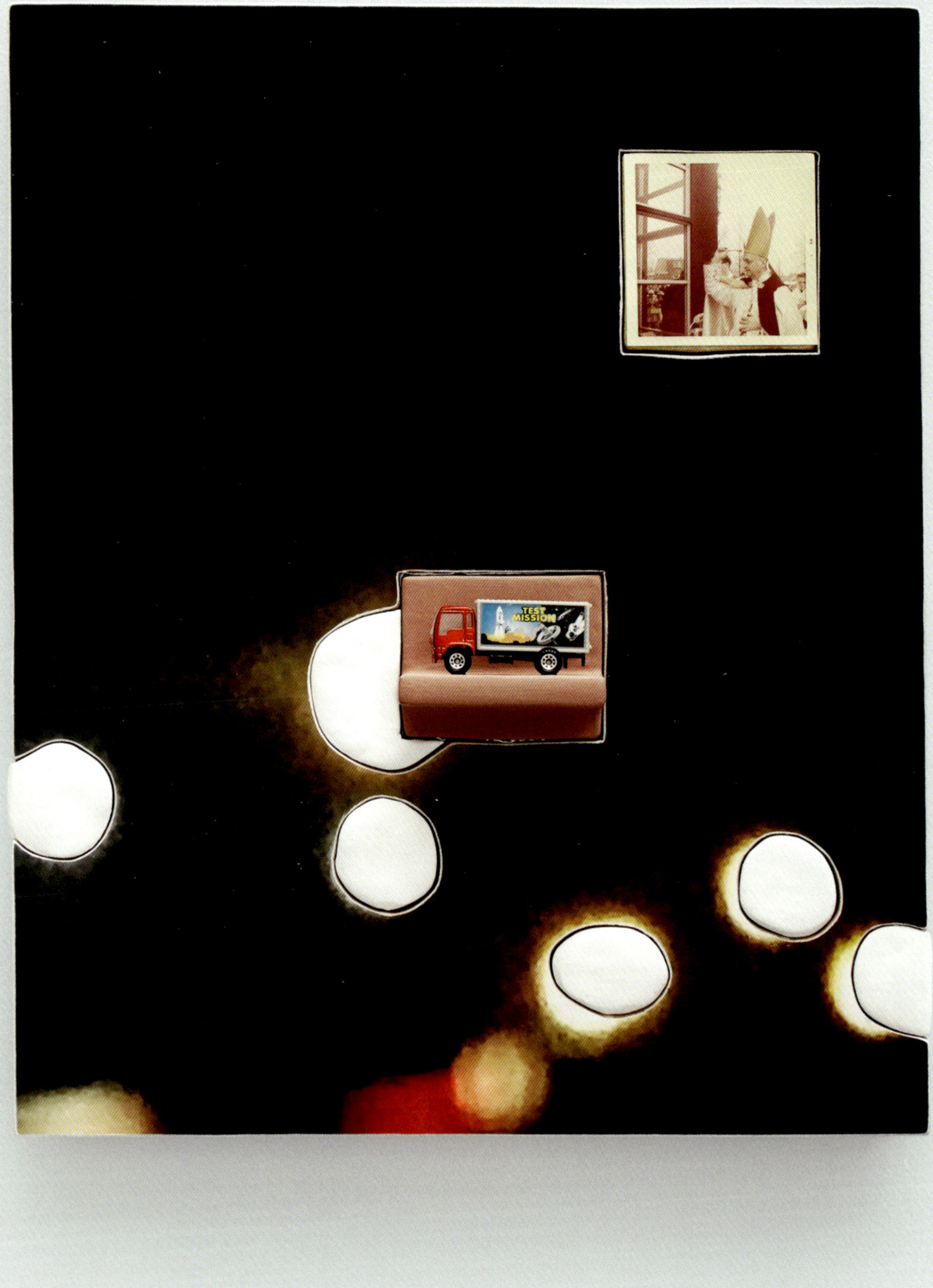
TEST
MISSION

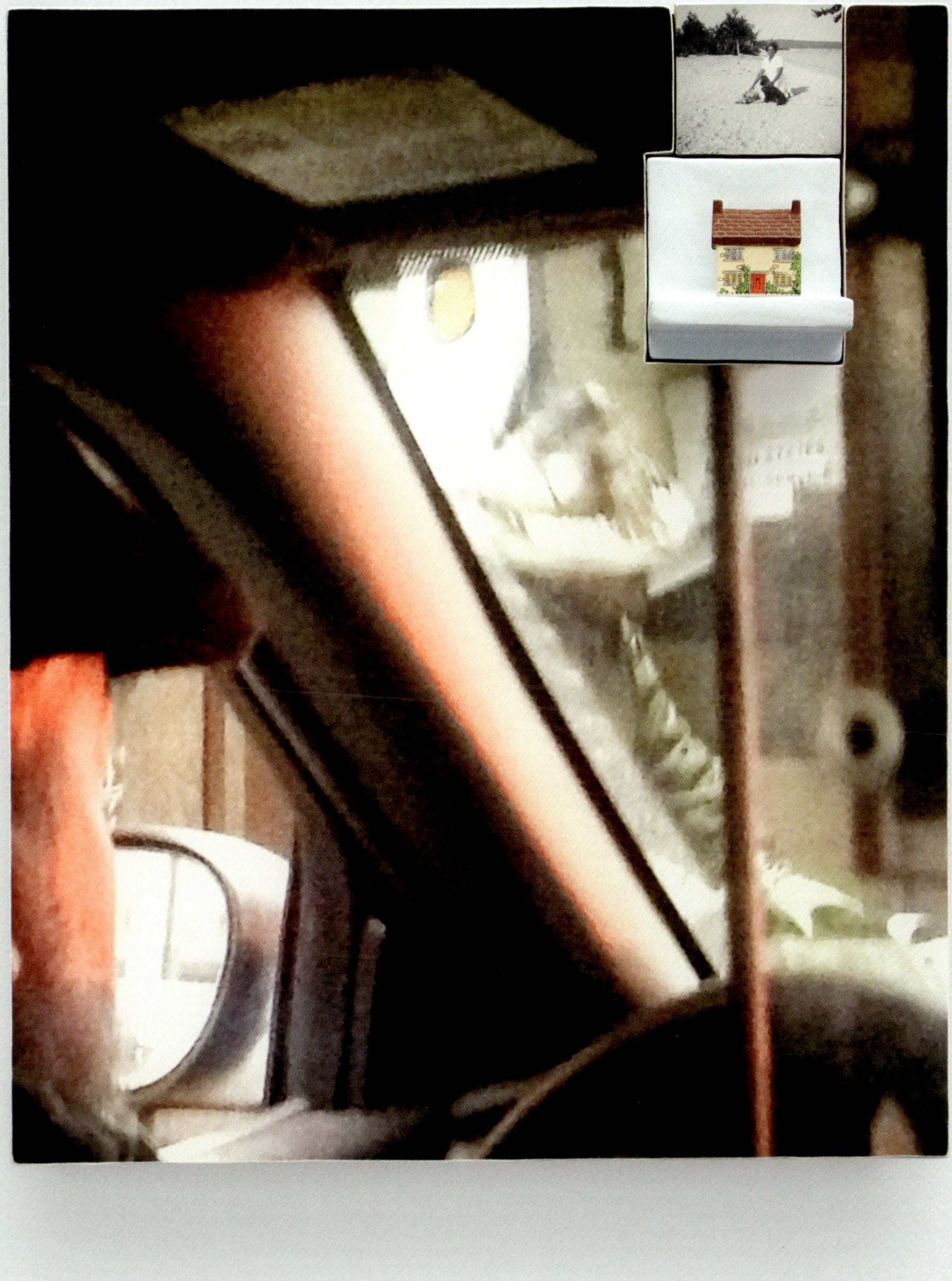

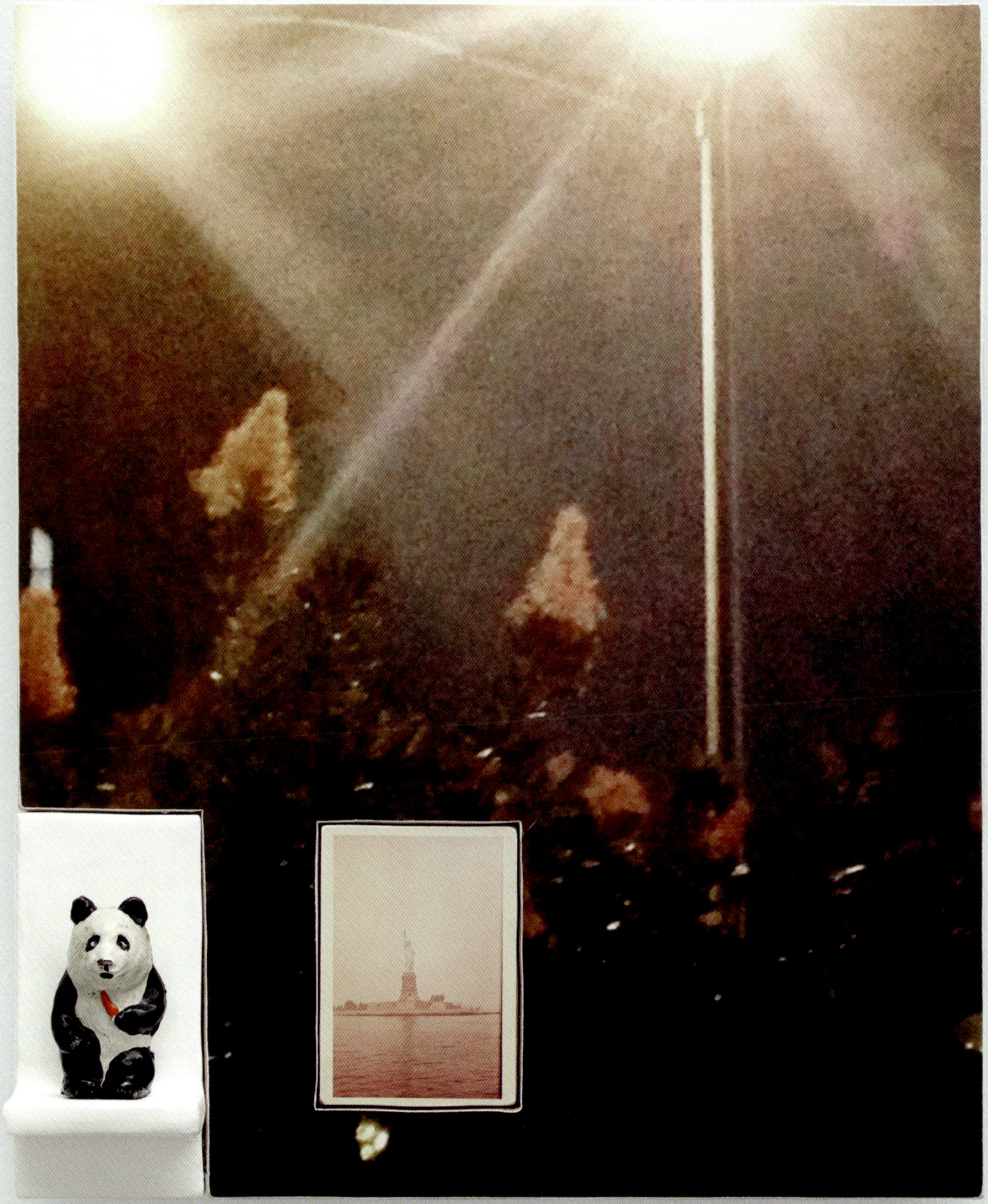

Sequence 8: Panels 24–27

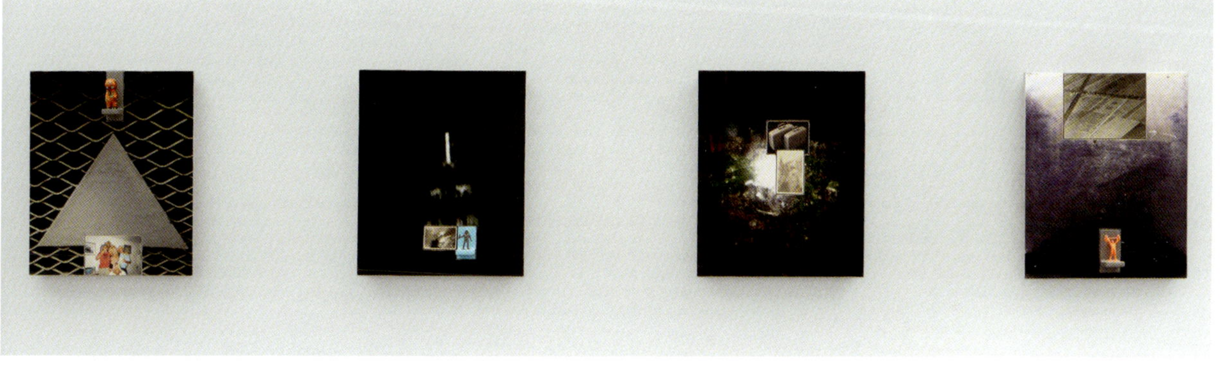

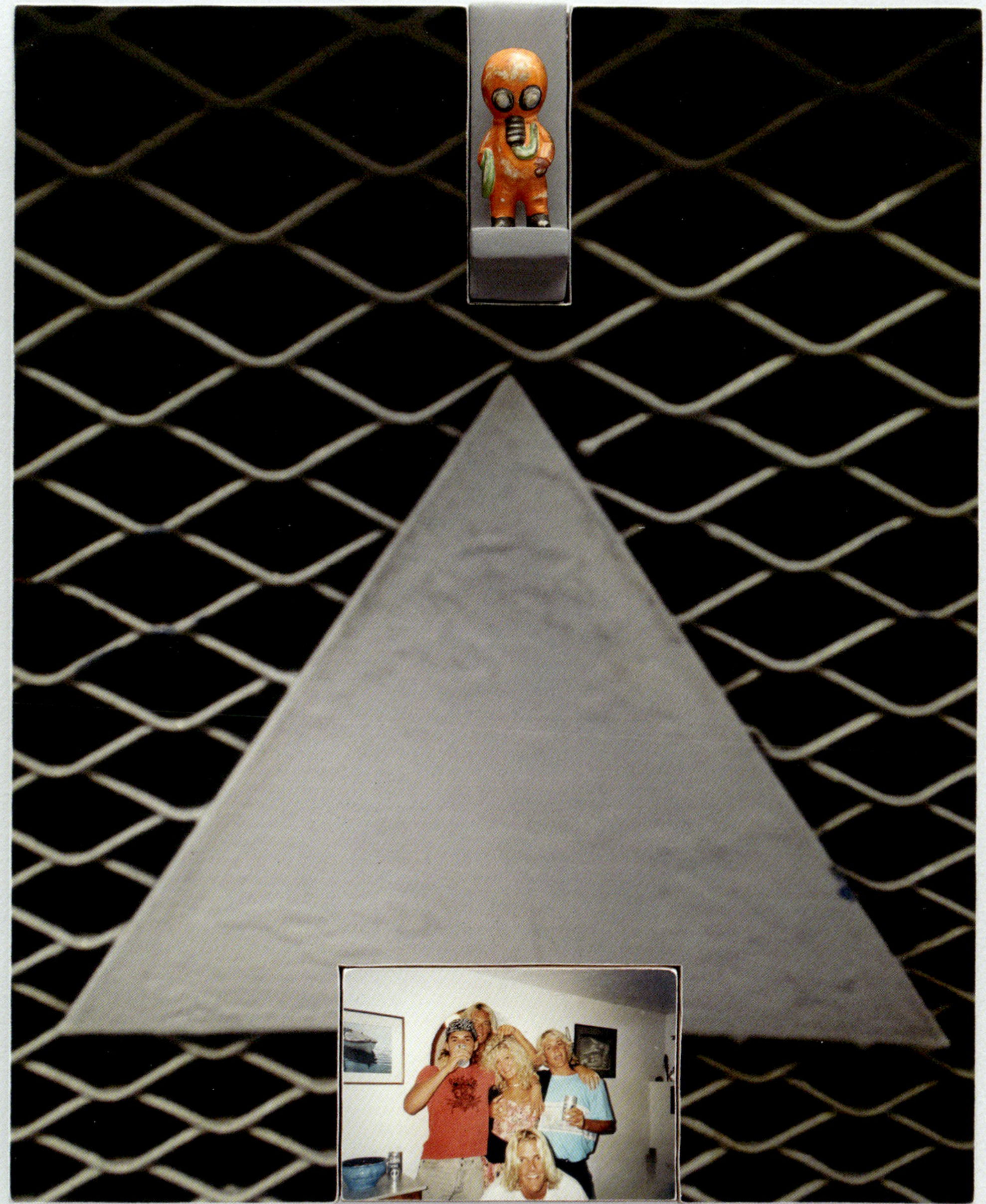

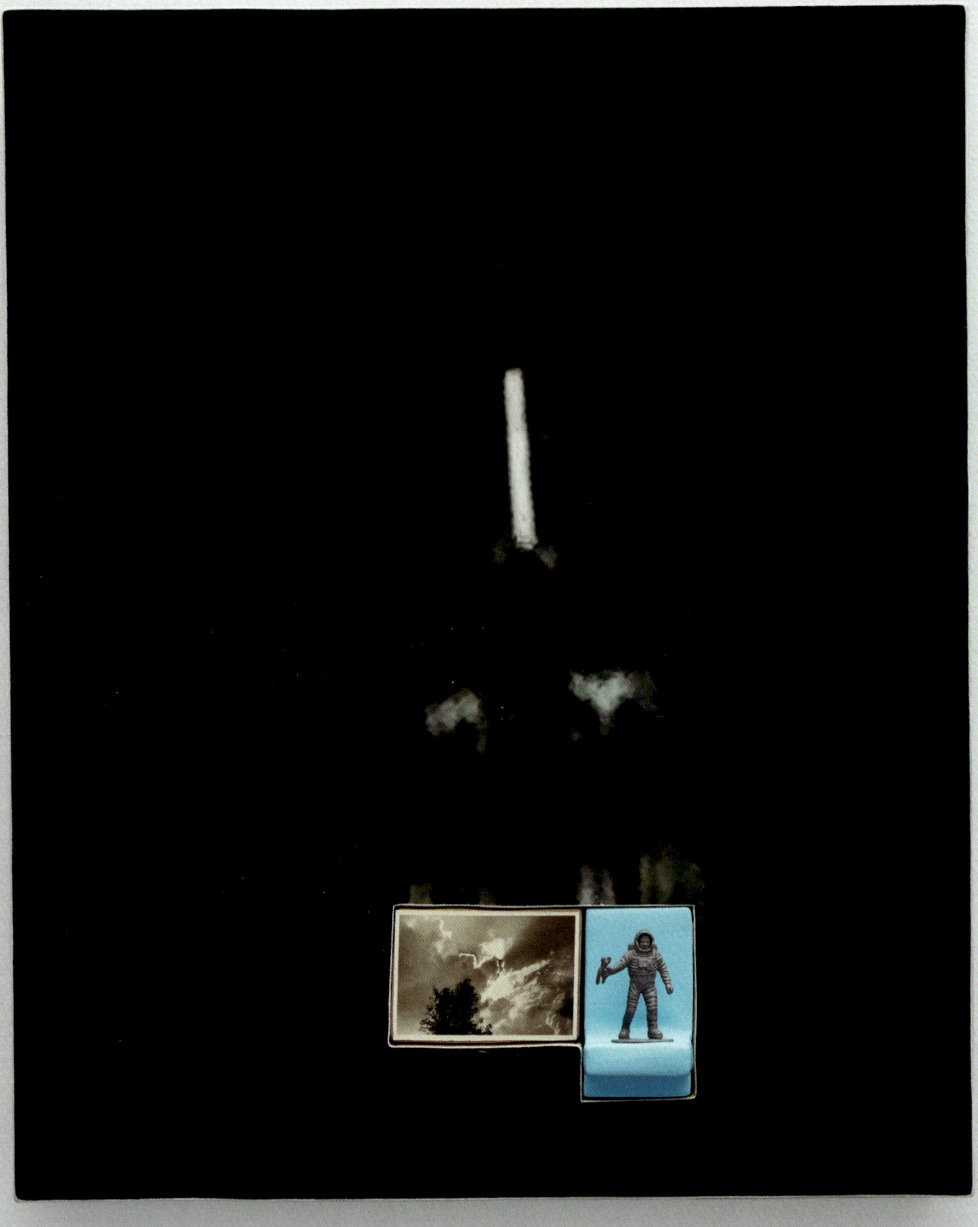

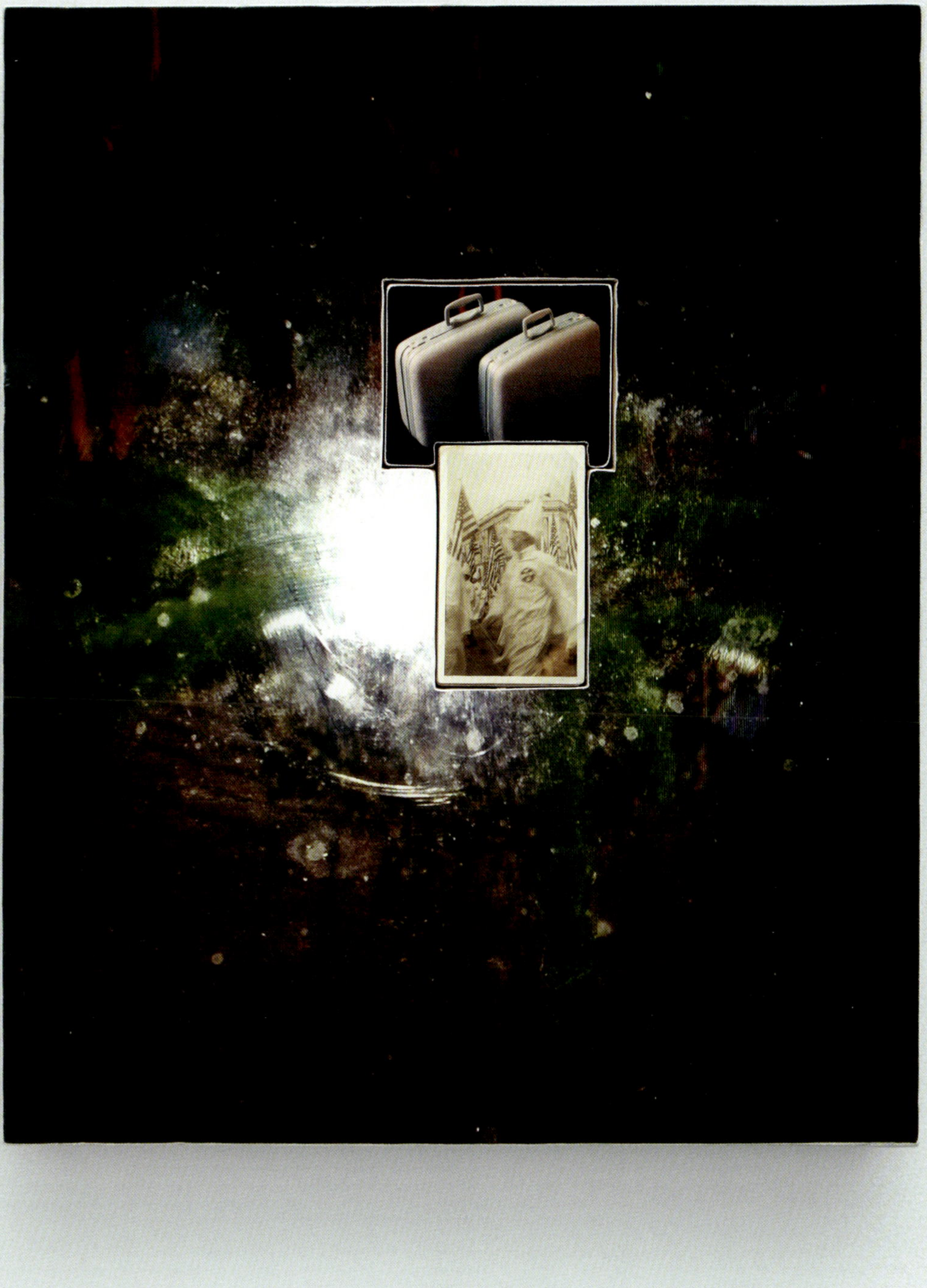

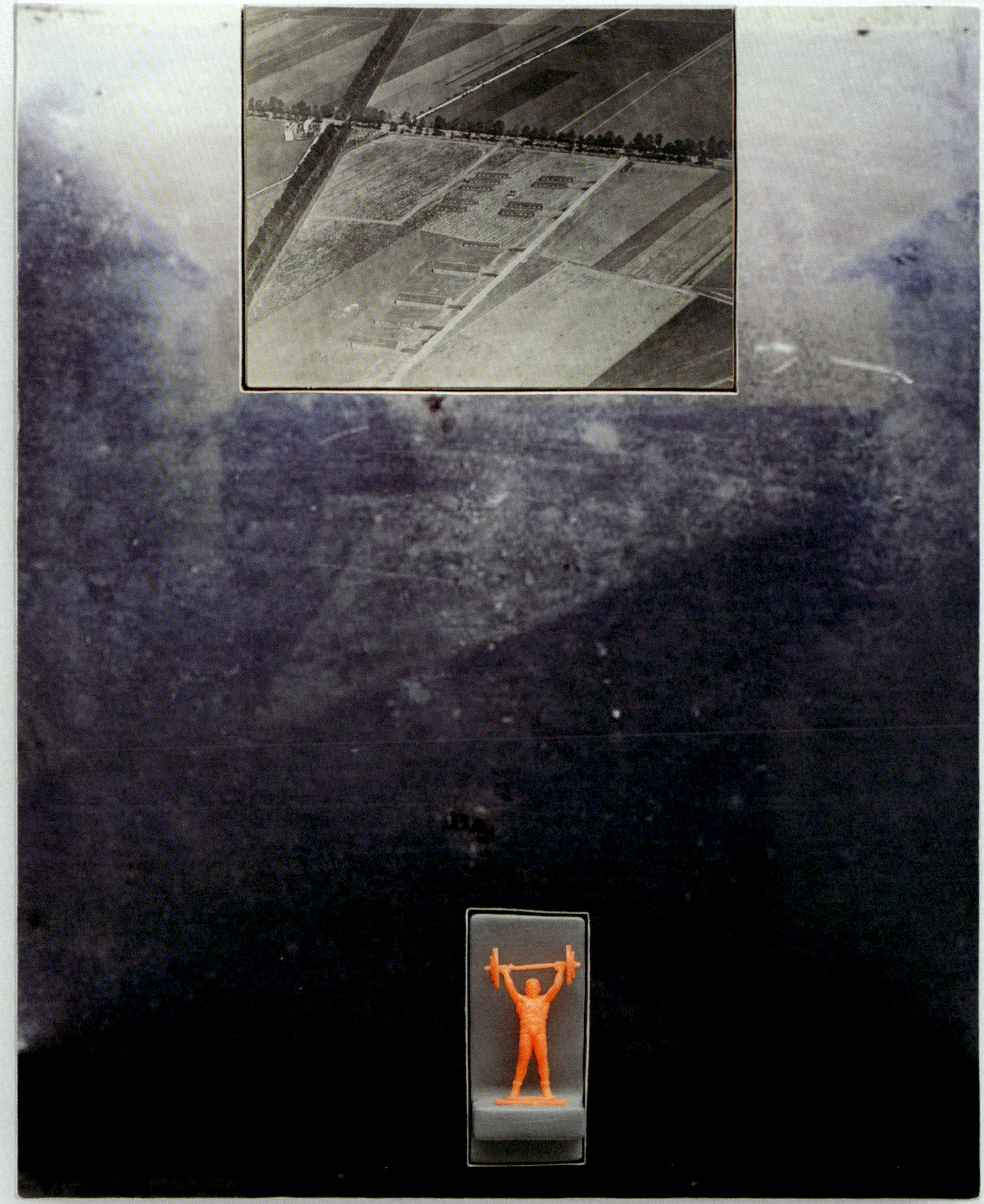

Sequence 9: Panels 28–31

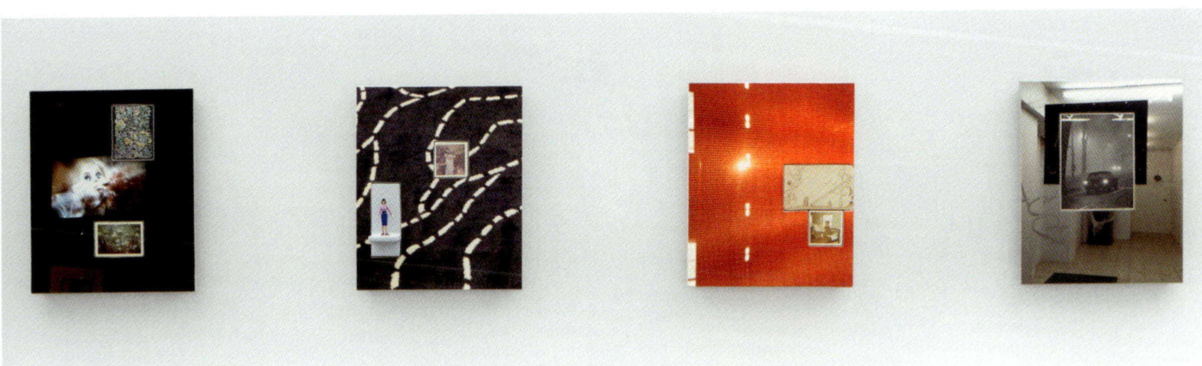

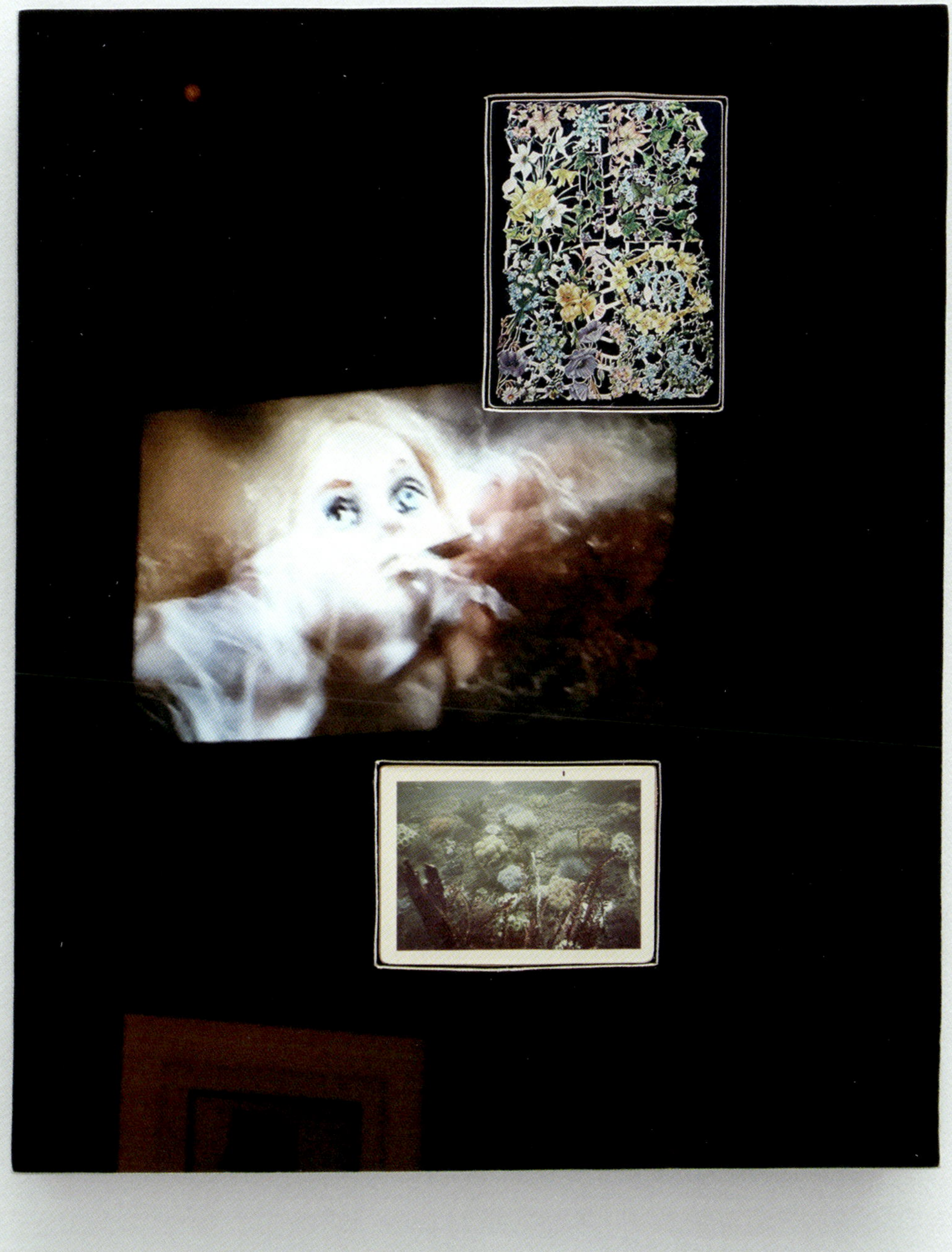

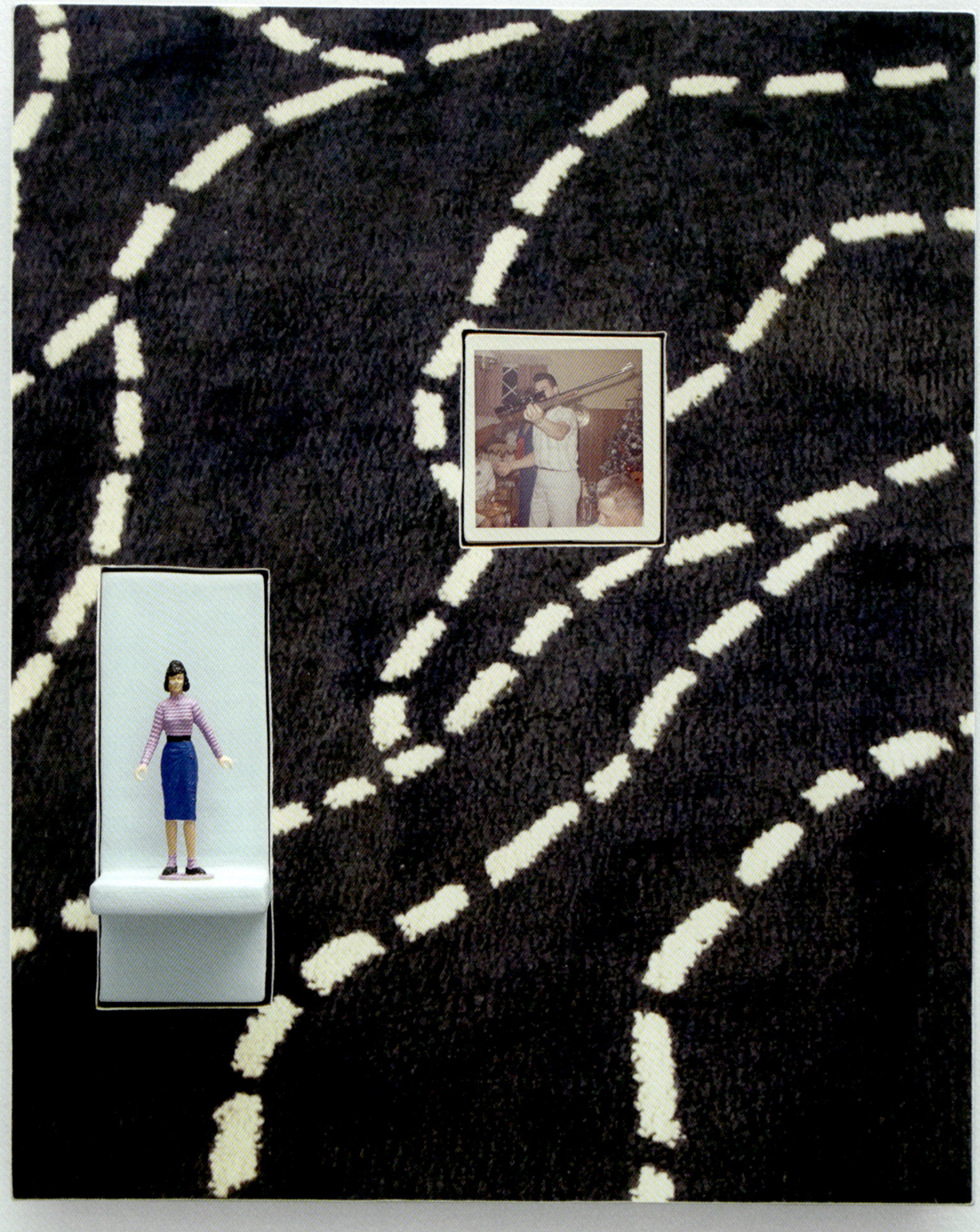

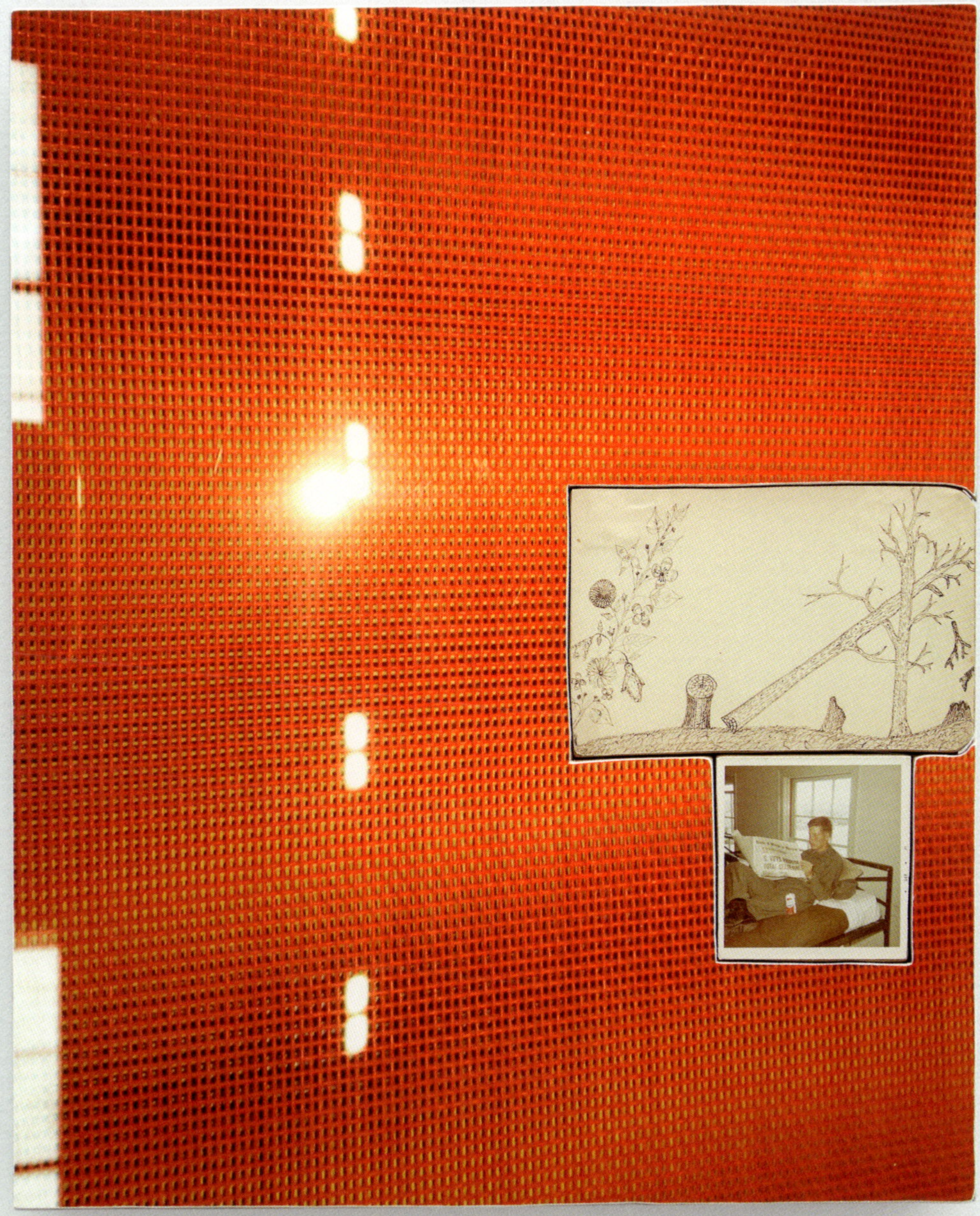

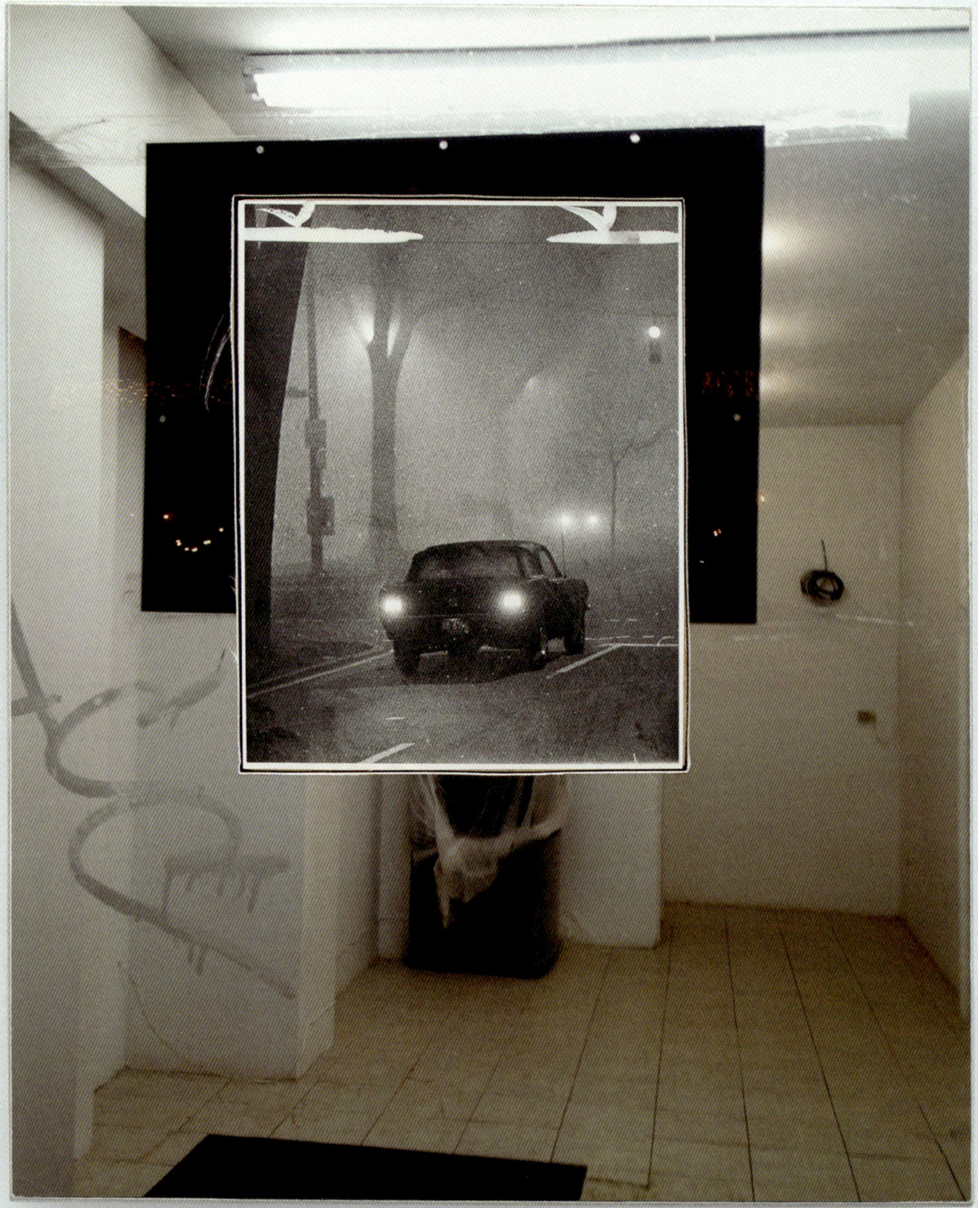

Sequence 10: Panels 32–35

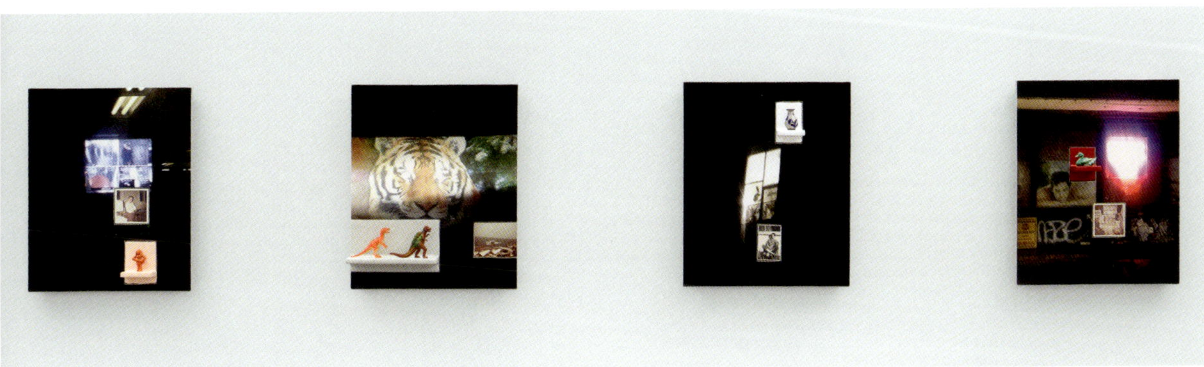

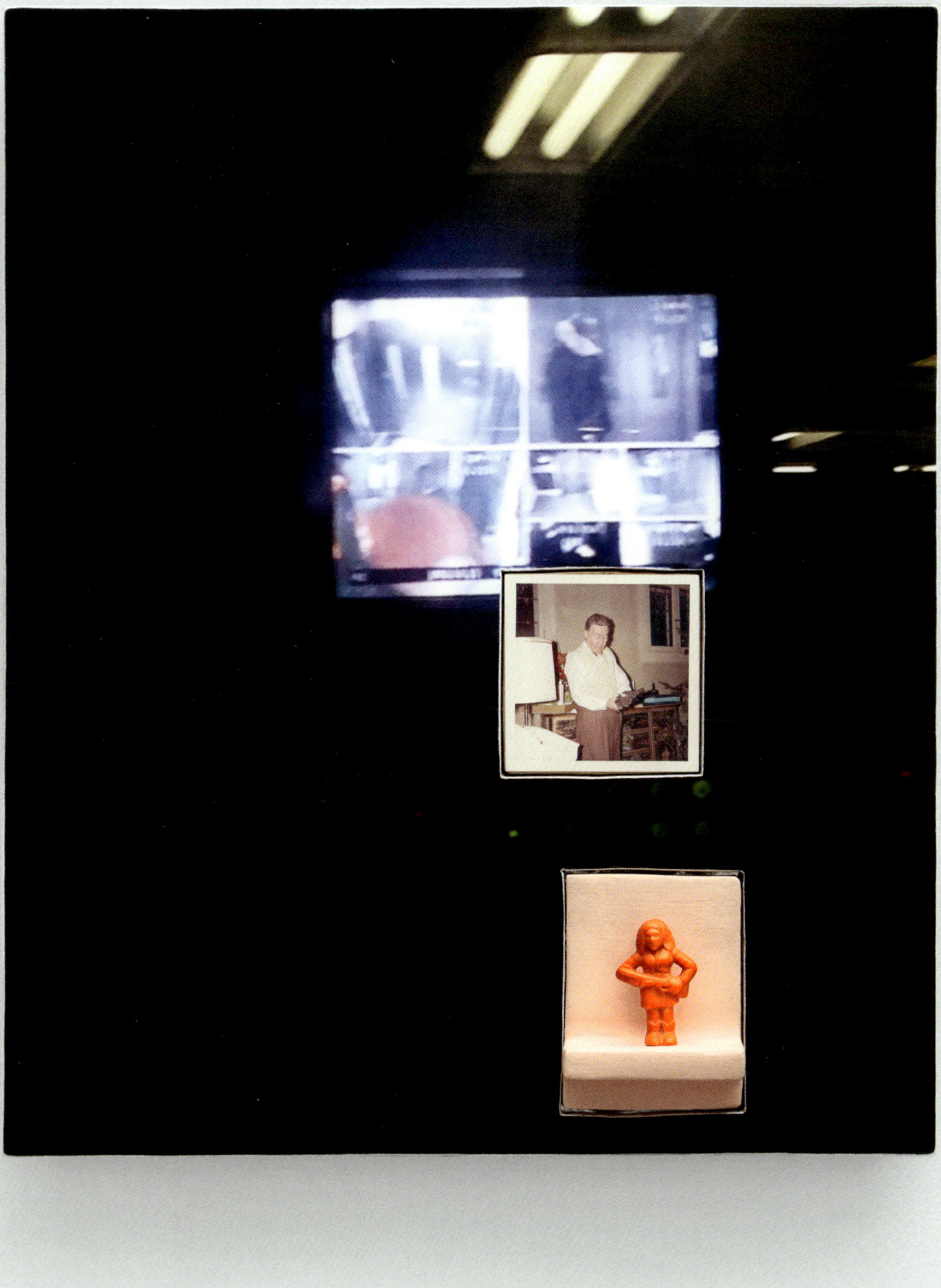

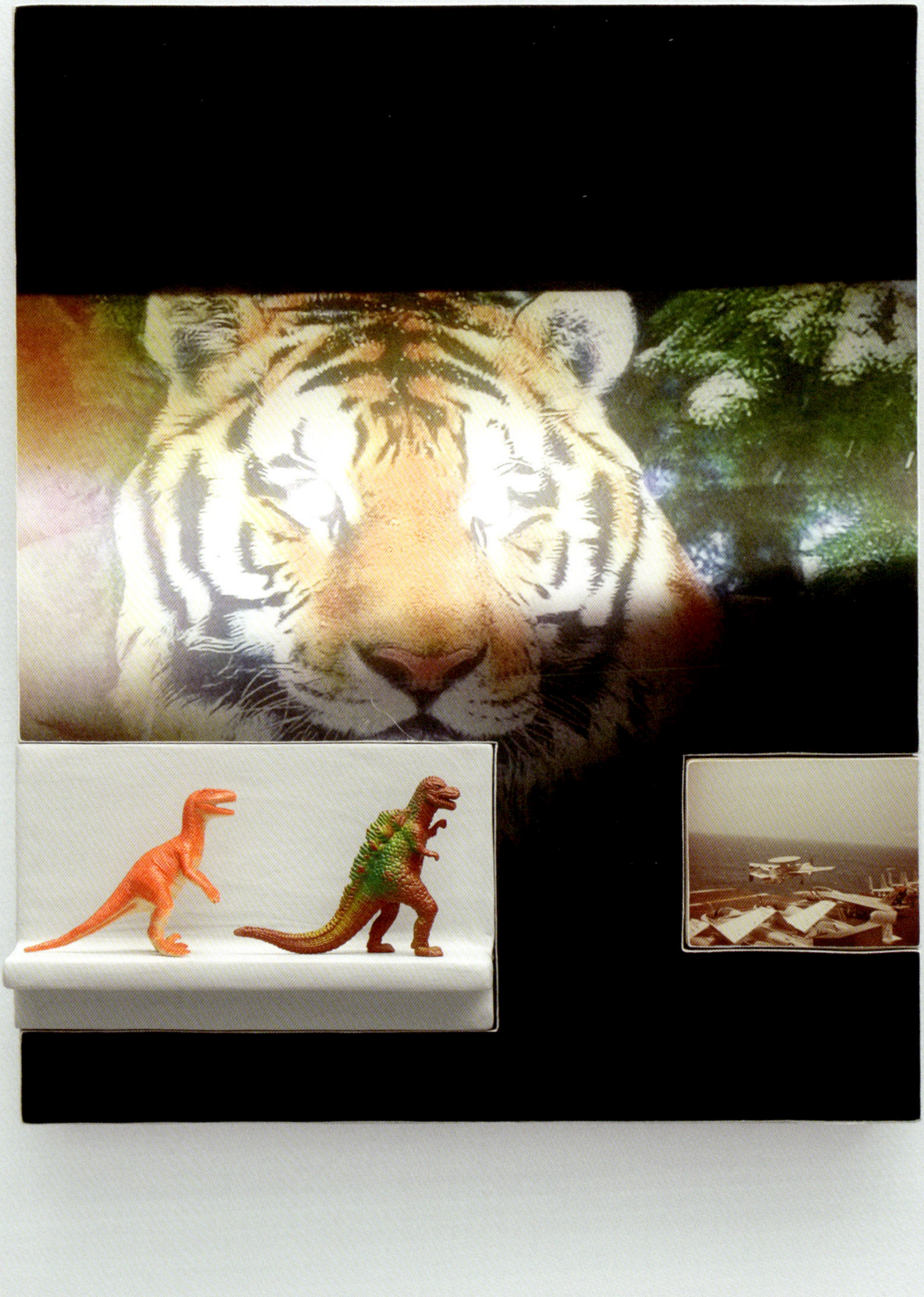

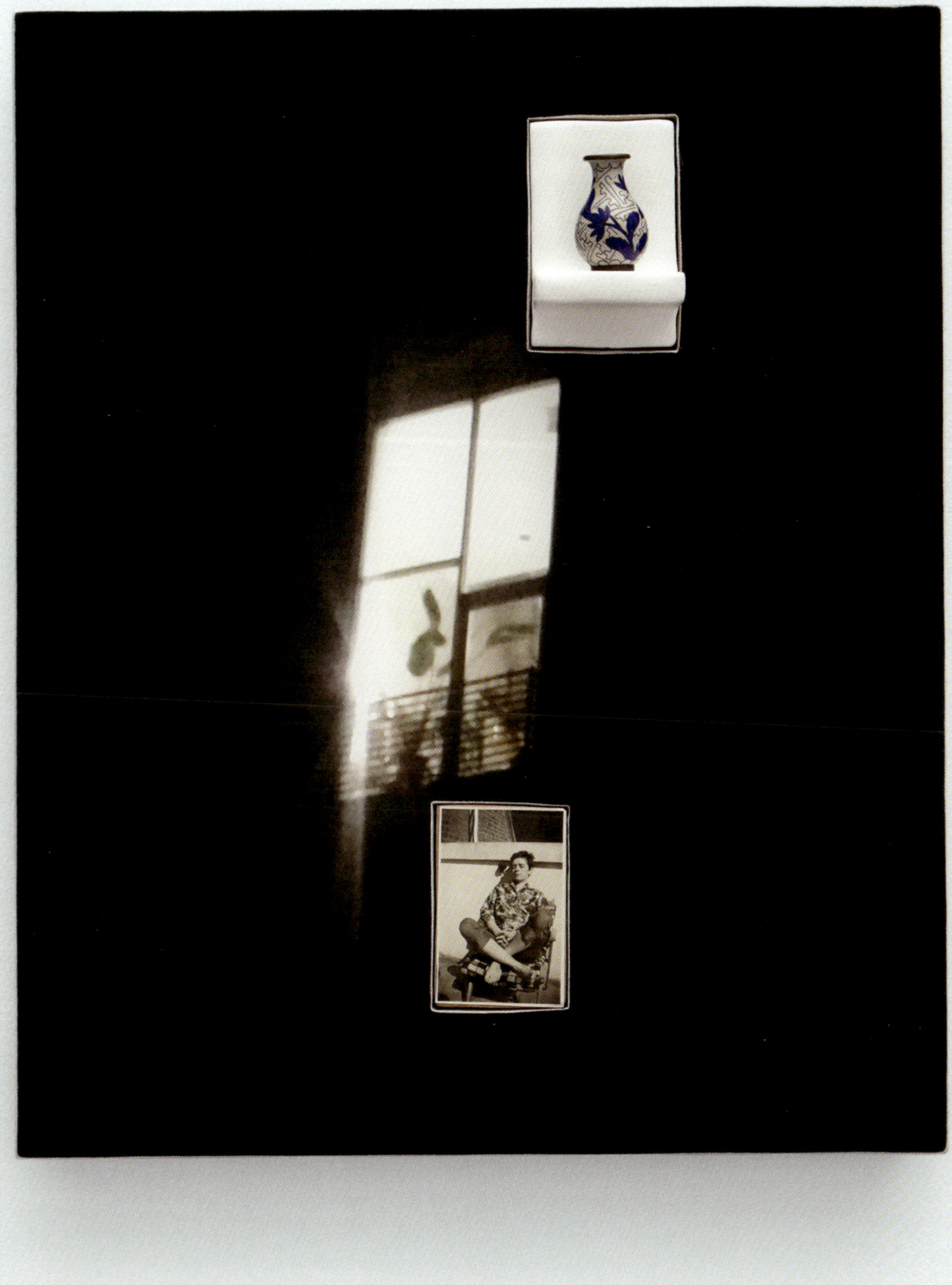

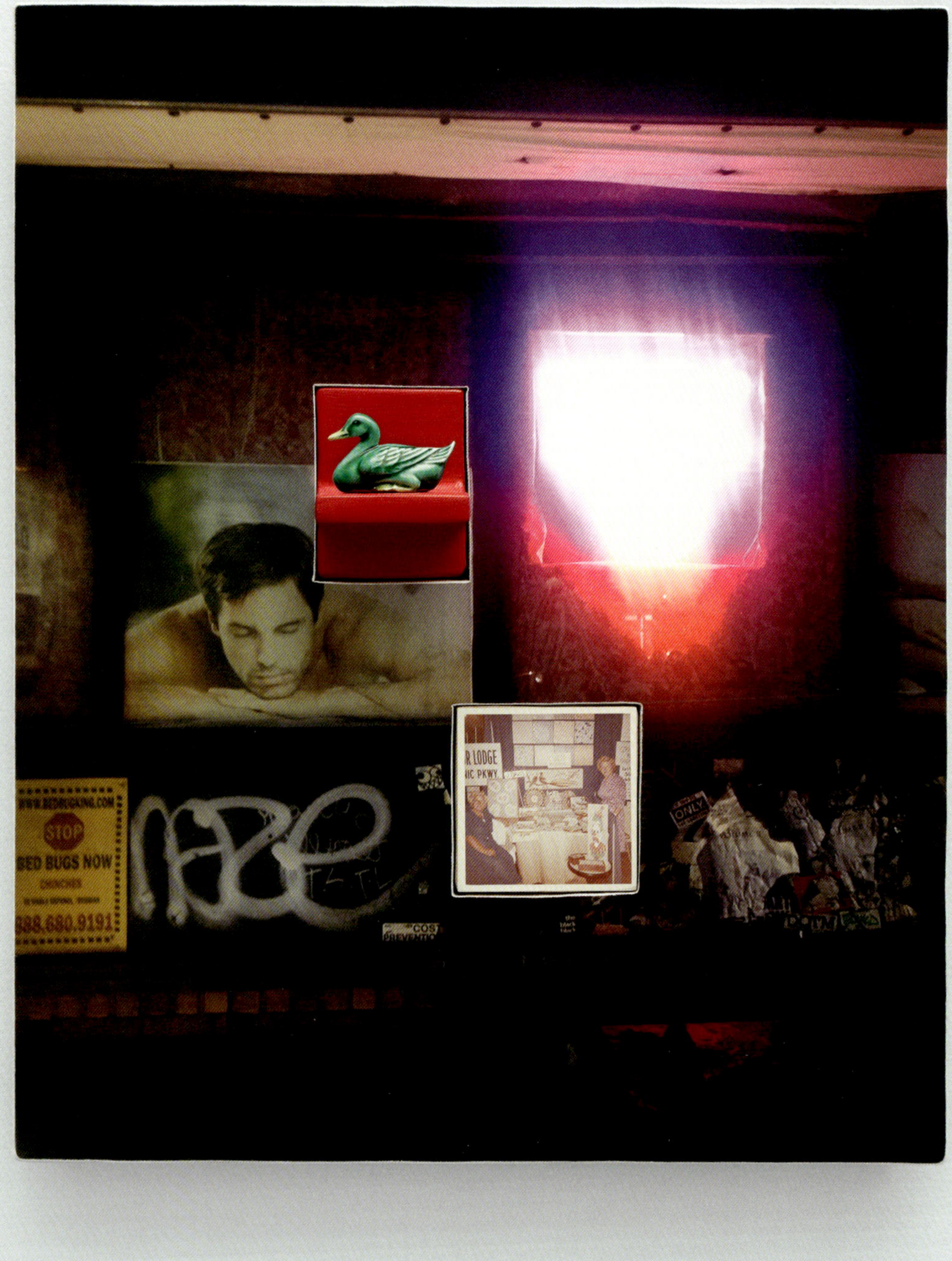
STOP
BED BUGS NOW
888.680.9191

Sequence 11: Panel 36

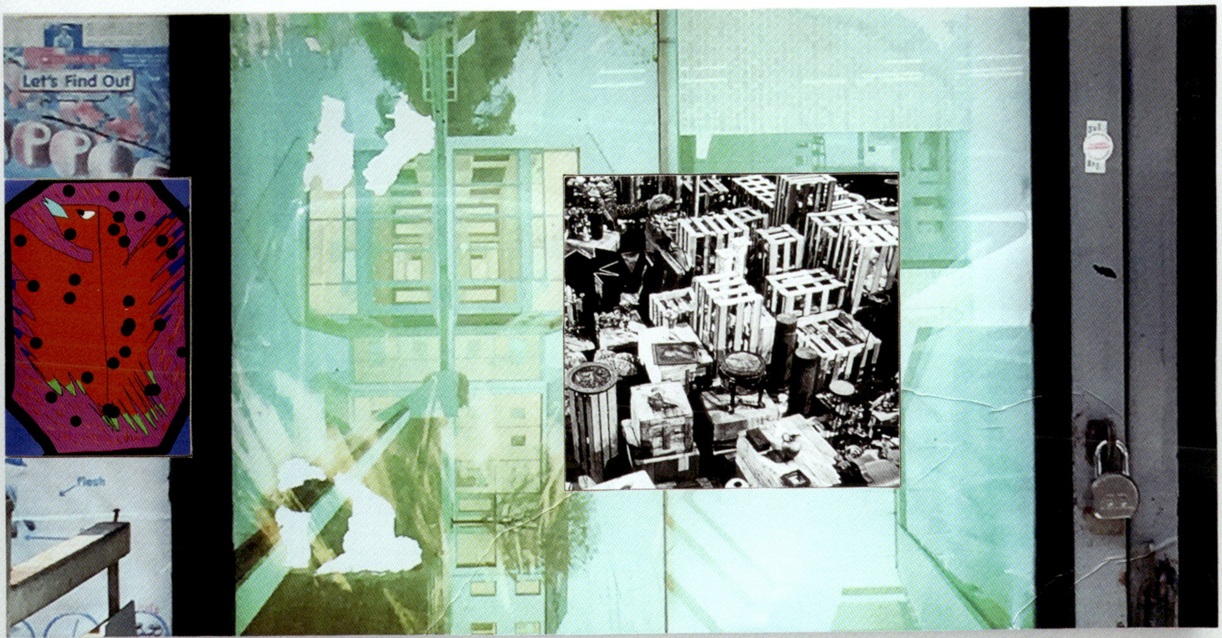
Let's Find Out
Flesh

Sequence 12: Panel 37

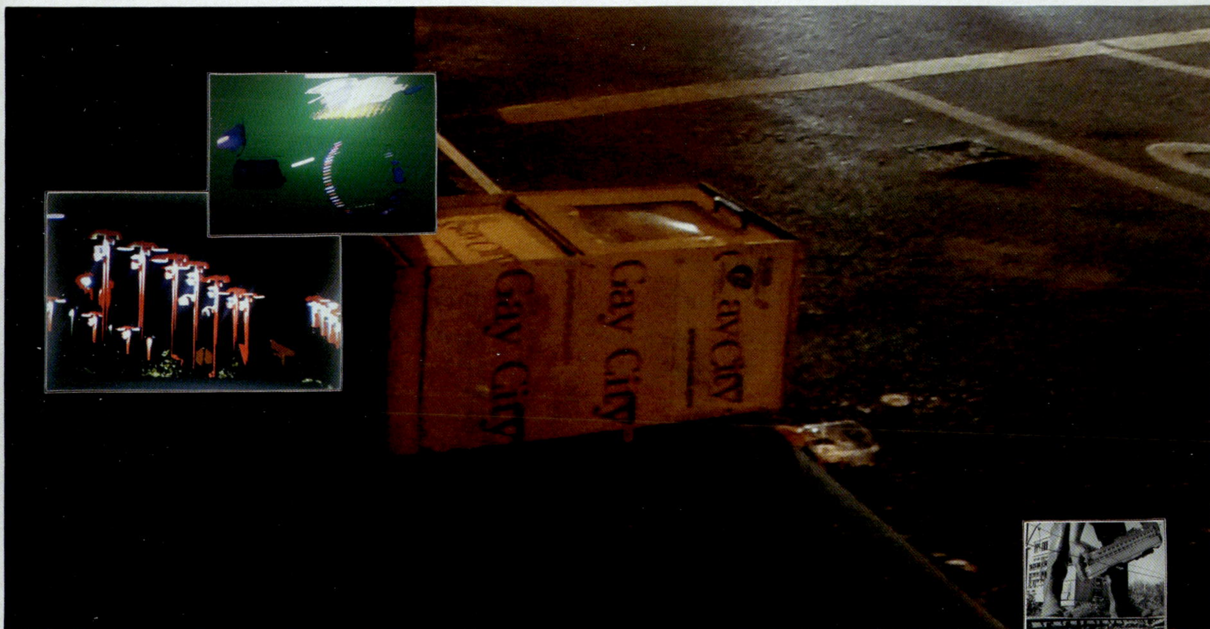
Gay City

Sequence 13: Panel 38

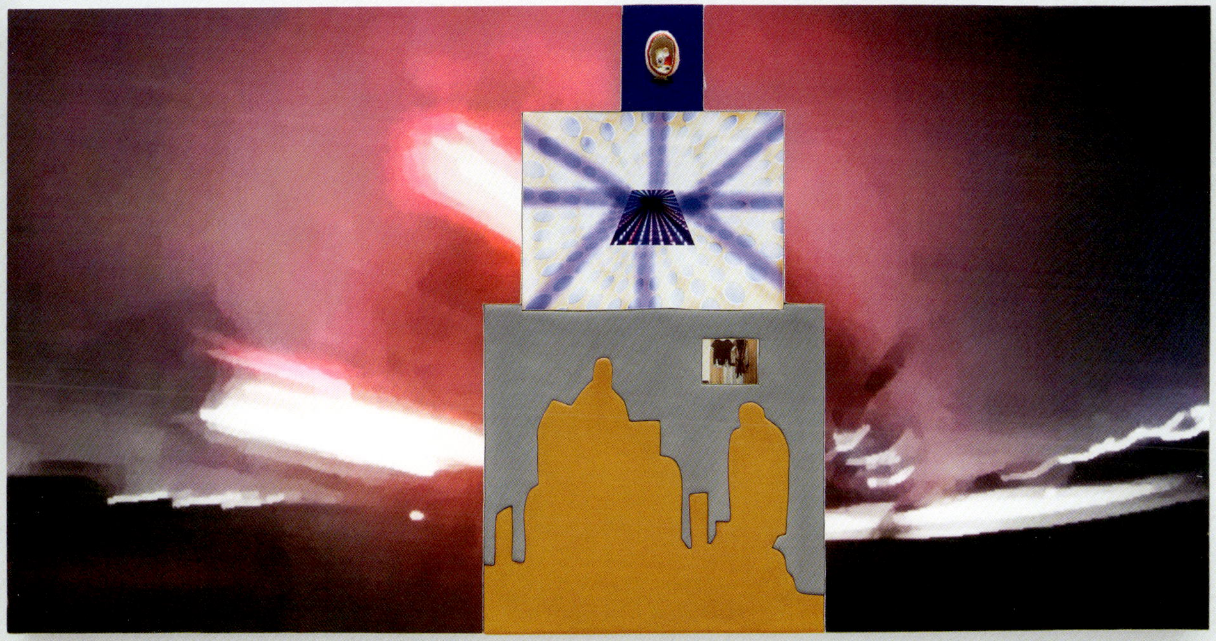

Sequence 14: Panel 39

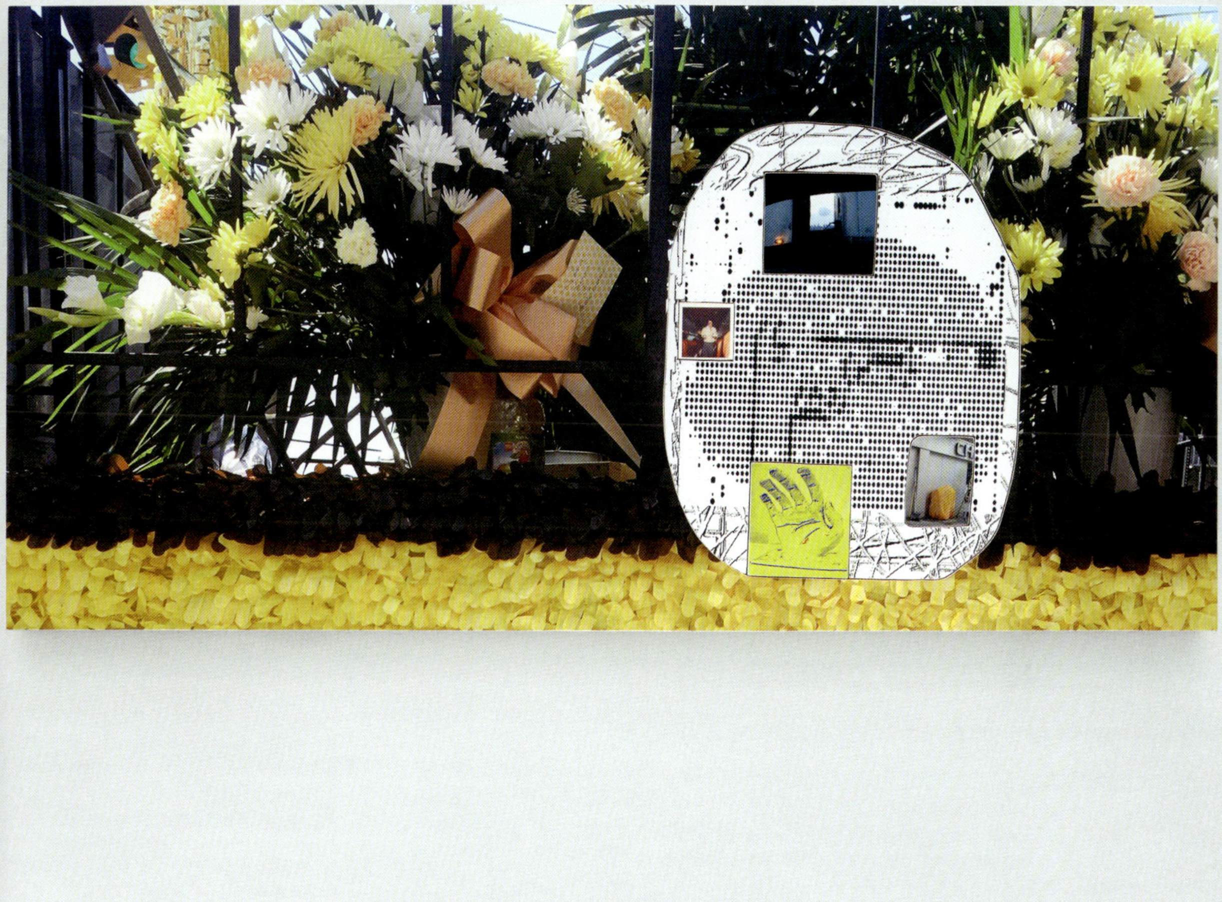

Sequence 15: Panel 40

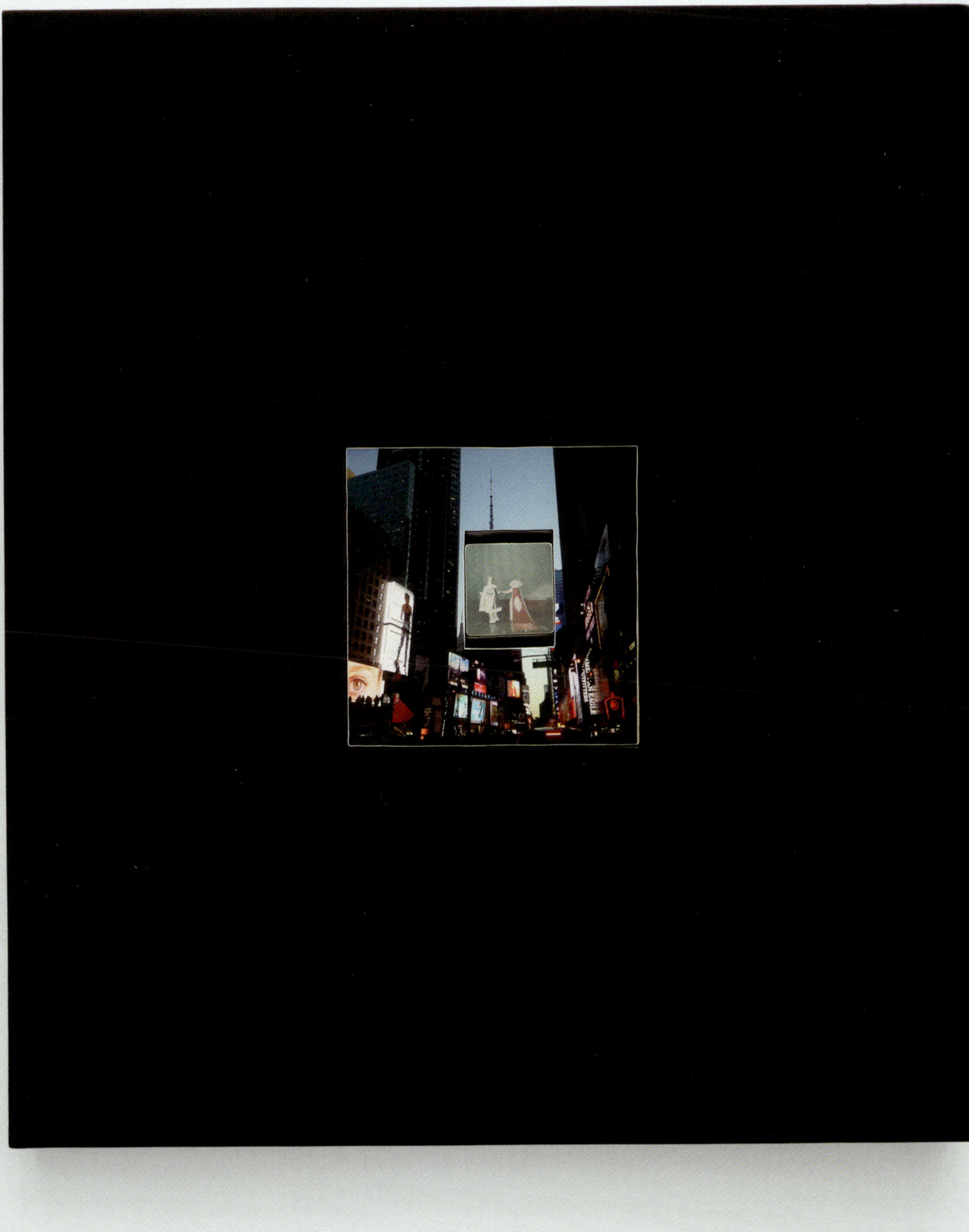

In Conversation

Julie Ault and Sadie Benning

Julie Ault and Sadie Benning

Recorded interview, January 31, 2017

JA I want to learn more about your day-to-day practice and your process. From what I've witnessed, you're always working through something that occupies you, whether in your studio or at home or elsewhere. You seem to readily generate ad hoc work space and a kind of thought bubble for yourself.

I've also been impressed by how you marshal content from your immediate surround and field of vision, wherever you are. You're continually sketching and visualizing, playing with materials, and experimenting with ways of giving form to your thoughts and insights.

SB I think that's accurate—the thought-bubble aspect of it, like imagining. Because I do feel like being creative—you're making a channel in your mind for things to happen so that you can have thoughts or ideas that are coming to you, but you have to create a space for them to exist, either through actively making things or through giving yourself time to not know what you're doing.

It takes a while to understand how things fit together. I often have lots of little parts. So it might be a drawing or fragments of a video. It might be different mediums that I'm working with. But it's the content that starts to build when I allow myself to experiment, and also just from doing mundane things, because so much of your daily experience is not making art. It's like having to pay a bill or whatever—getting a parking ticket. That's the bureaucracy of living or the frustrations politically that are going on around one's life that start to interface with this desire to make something as well. So these things fuse together over time.

In part, that transitory feeling of being wherever you are and still allowing yourself the space to think or work is from personal experience, of having always been traveling around between family members and friends. My mom worked at a hotel doing construction and we were always in a different hotel room every night. So I would deal with, regularly, the transitory state of the hotel and just making do in that in-between state.

And some of this is class-based. There's a desire to make do with scraps, the things that you have around you, whether it's a phone book or a newspaper or pencils or whatever you might have access to that's immediate. Also growing up around grandparents who lived through the Depression and wouldn't throw anything away. I have a bit of a hoarder mentality of keeping materials around me that I think I might use or might become necessary at some point.

JA I didn't know that about your mother. I knew you traveled between different family members when you were growing up, but it sounds like it was more than a schedule. Adapting to and establishing a personal space within these various public situations was a way of life that you imbued with invention.

SB I'm also thinking about being different, being queer, being transgender, and the need to look at the world and reinterpret it so that it makes more sense to me. Because so many things are set up in ways that deny people their consciousness or their humanity. Making art allows you to deal with that invention or to reinterpret the cultural material around you.

JA I'm wondering how you experience focus.

SB I think it has changed over time. For example, when I was really young and I first started making videos, I would shoot them all in camera and edit them almost as fast as they were to watch—maybe ten minutes. Or some of those videos, I waited for a year and a half to piece together in a weird way. The first video I made I shot in my bedroom in Milwaukee, but then went to visit my dad, and I took the camera with me on the plane and shot the very end of it in California on the same tape because I didn't know how to edit yet. When I began to develop a technical sense of editing, I started working on much more involved projects that sometimes took five or six years to edit.

I realized then that I wanted to be making things that were not using technology, that were using my hands and that were more immediate, like drawing could be. Something that could interject another space to be thinking in alongside this other time frame that seemed much longer and more involved.

Also it felt depressing to be dependent on Sony and Apple, these corporate superpowers that could decide at any moment to kill your medium—video wasn't a stable medium, and as a consumer you had no real protection, you were under the thumb of whatever direction they wanted to take you in. So it was liberating to decide I could work with a paintbrush and gouache instead.

I guess I go back and forth between different types of attention spans. But I think regarding focus, one of the things I find myself doing—I don't know if it's meditative exactly, but I go into a sense of focusing where I'm present and I'm also not present. Like when I'm on the train but I'm kind of in a trance. It's also an experience of living with technology where we are multitasking and doing things simultaneously. It's the experience of interacting all day with phones and the internet. Of having to shift focus all the time between these different scales of thinking, like things that are cognitive, things that seem so much outside the self as well.

JA It sounds like you have a repertoire of concentration modes and they happen organically, not that you choose one or the other.

SB Also I have a unique history in that I started making videos when I was fifteen, and so the time period at which I was starting to generate ideas—I wasn't quite formulated in terms of who I was. I was coming to terms. There was content that was personal within the earlier video work that I made, but I also realized over time that a lot of what I thought was literal about identity then was actually much more complicated and abstract. Or I wasn't necessarily even self-aware enough at the time to be able to be truthful. I learned from that time that even when I think I'm being really focused and attuned, I still don't totally know.

I think sometimes that's complicated, because in the world, especially having taught in art schools, you want students to be able to talk about what their ideas mean and not just be like, "Oh, this is nonsense, it doesn't mean anything." But I do think there's a huge part of our brains where we don't understand. I like that relationship between what I know and what I don't know. And I try to make room for both of those things to coexist when I'm making something, because in the end I do become more aware.

JA Does your early video work still unfold and teach you things about yourself?

SB Honestly, I haven't looked at it recently. But when I have, I feel a couple of things: I'm amazed at how easily it could have been that I just didn't show anybody this, or that something else could have happened. The narrative could have been very different, especially being a teenager and how insecure one is at that age. And yet I also had access to artists and friends who were interested in looking at things. Ultimately, I think the reason that I started to make things is I wanted to have a reason to talk to people about ideas. Otherwise, growing up in Milwaukee and living there, there's a way that if you didn't try to create something as a way to reach people, you might feel trapped.

So it resonates with me now that there are all these other virtual ways of interacting, it just seems more incredible to me that I reached people the way I did—with VHS tapes.

JA That's great. It doesn't sound like you have the cringe factor of early work.

SB Oh, no. I definitely have that, too. [*Laughs*] I think the thing that's the most complicated for me about the early work I made is I've gone through all kinds of periods of feeling different about it. And even now, sometimes it's hard for me to physically represent it—I've changed a lot. I'm transgender and I identify differently. And maybe I didn't actually identify so differently then, but I didn't have language to discuss it. So it's not exactly cringe factor, but it's almost out-of-body. Like, I don't totally understand that person in the same way anymore, or that performer.

JA It has its life, and it has a voice and a vocabulary that is specific to a time. And the fact that it's still speaking to people is great.

SB I think also time is necessary in order to get to a point where a conversation can develop about how to think about one's own practice, especially when it comes to identity. People need to evolve. The world has to evolve, too.

JA I've been thinking about your adaptable relationship to mode and how you incorporate multiple ways of working at once and

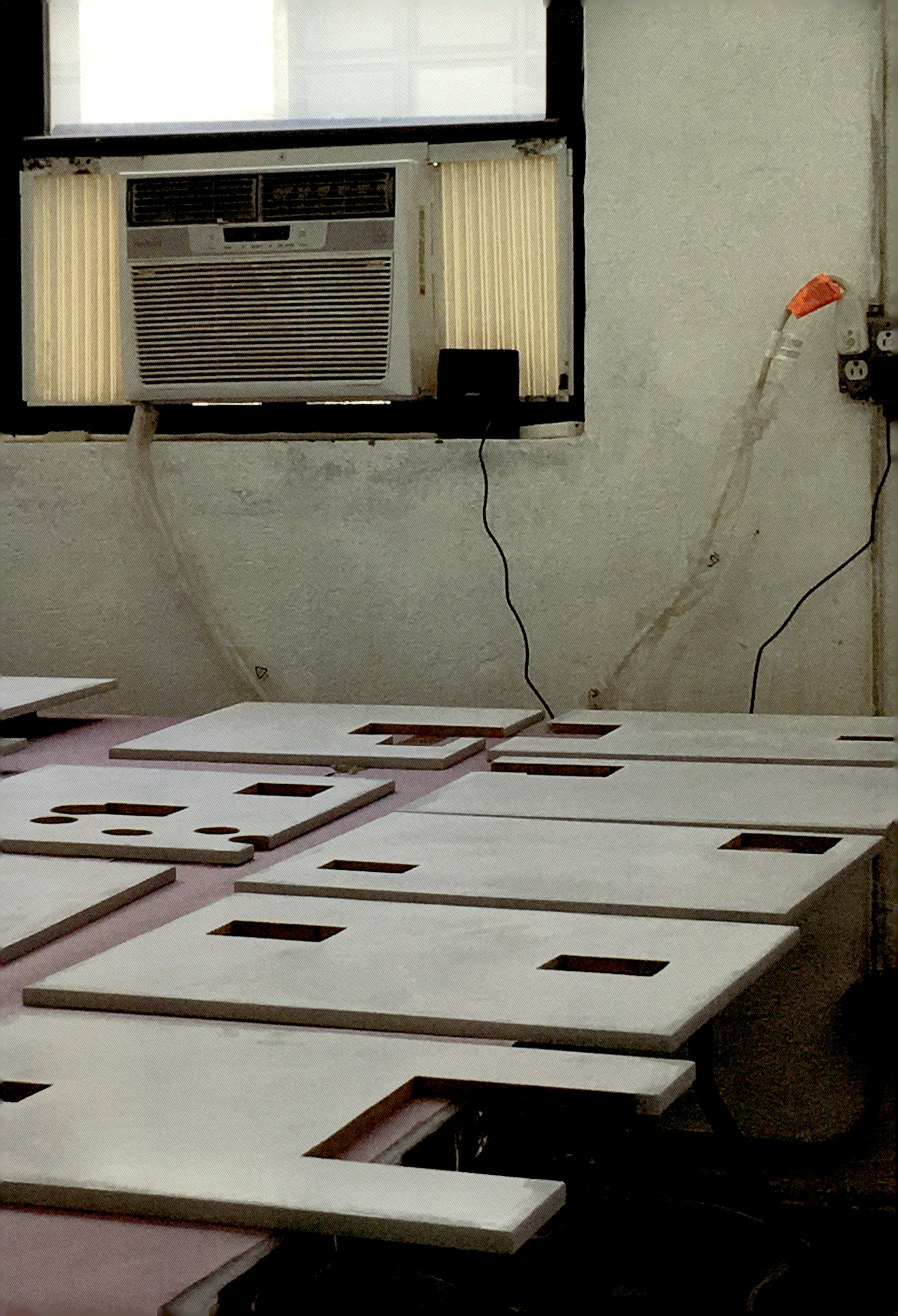

come up with crossbred forms. Your flexible relation to method and the composite forms you develop are represented in critical realms as an unusual position with respect to media within art and seen as a way of escaping categorization. But we know that isolating media into separate histories, sites, and economies is an artificial, institutionalizing device. It's a means of managing the messiness of culture and our brains, and the perceived riskiness of infinite crossbreeding. Isolating media is also useful for manufacturing symbolic value and authority.

Your versatility is not strategic. I don't regard it as a bid for the art world, despite the fact that it is a model that inspires. I think of your relationship to form as innate, in that what you do as an artist seems to mirror how you exist in and use and take part in culture. Your relationship to form seems—I'm using the word once again—*organic*.

SB [*Laughs*]

JA It seems to indicate realism rather than social idealism. It shows how culture is.

SB Using hybrid mediums or one form to think through another form feels instinctive or organic, as you say. I prefer to try to understand one medium through another. Somehow the relationship between forms allows me to access something else completely different. A lot of the people I know who make things don't want to necessarily segregate their mediums or ideas. It can feel oppressive—but, as I was saying before, this is also about a kind of experience in the world. I want to identify with people who are different from me. I want to understand relationships between things. And so that's one of the reasons I might want to think about video through painting or painting through photography. These mediums might not just merge into each other—they can still retain aspects of themselves. It's not like I'm melting them down into a blended gumbo or something.

JA There are so many ways that politics are part of your work. Regardless of what media you use, there's a visibly hands-on or homemade disposition. And across the various directions and turns, your work always feels personal, which I see as political. In much of your work, I sense the hand, I sense a body; I feel a mind, a sense of humor, closeness. And I discern compassion. I don't perceive an investment on your part in the artwork as a bearer of the artist's aura. And as far as I know there's no outsize ego behind the curtain. But your address is always personal.

Whatever of your work I've seen arouses a physical relationship in advance of a metaphysical one. And the physicality feels political and generous to me, especially in these digital, hyperautomated times.

SB It's been illuminating to transition between shooting videos and moving toward painting and object-making. Seeing a video in a theater or seeing a painting in a gallery is a very different physical experience for an audience member. A lot of the work that I currently make is hand-built; it oscillates between representation and abstraction. When I took away the moving image from my practice and started painting, there were new limitations. It was like, "OK, how do you make sound or say words? How do you deal with time in these different mediums?" The painting might not literally have the ability to talk like a film does. But yet it still has something to say, you know?

In the *Shared Eye* show, I was interested in how perception is constructed. We see things the way we do because of an amalgamation of realities, but in part because of how we have been taught to perceive things based on our families and the greater culture around us.

JA How were you working on this before it was a body of work and there was the framework of *Shared Eye*, when there was an out-of-focus mixture of things and ideas and glimmers taking shape?

SB I was taking lots of photographs and had started to experiment with miniatures and found photographs, making works that incorporated the different found materials with painted and sculptural elements.

So I was starting to think within the realm of combining these materials. I often make mock-ups—versions out of paper first. A lot of ideas happen in what I think of as preproduction, where you're editing and working out the scale things will be.

Some of these decisions start to make sense when you have a location—when you know when and where the work is going to exist. And those coordinates help you evolve what you've already been making. Also I consistently draw in a bunch of notebooks. I don't necessarily look at those notebooks for three or four years, and then I look back at them and there will be a succession of maybe twelve drawings. It's like an idea was going from one page to the next, and it feels threaded, like it needs to stay together. Then I'll pull those things out and start working with them.

For *Shared Eye*, I was working on all these miniature mock-ups, often on the subway. I like being in transitory spaces when I'm working. I've always liked to have a lot of noise around me or a lot of things happening, a lot of activity. It helps me concentrate. And so I often make mock-ups while riding around on the train. Then I look through them later and edit them into something of a structure.

For *Shared Eye*, there was the particular location of the Renaissance Society in Chicago as the first venue for the work. I lived in Chicago for seventeen years. So when I went and looked at the space, it made me think about the past but also what was happening in the world currently. There was the lead-up to the 2016 election between Trump and Clinton—it had been several years of campaigning and extreme political polarization. Sexism and racism obviously predate the election, but suddenly there were more platforms for normalizing white supremacy, misogyny, xenophobia—straight-up criminality. That was the temperature when I was generating the work.

The show was going to open a week after the election, and I didn't know who was going to win. I wanted to deal with some of the atmosphere of that time. The weird thing was, I had already been creating that work. I was fielding it as a response to what I was sensing. So when I started to pull work out and edit, there was a lot that was already there. It's not like I had to insinuate it.

JA You and others talking about the show have mentioned the relation of *Shared Eye* to the deep polarization and uncertainty at hand with the campaigns and election. I feel that in the work. A sinister undercurrent emerges in some of the imagery and associations. But when were things ever sure? I don't think anything has ever been politically dependable in my lifetime. The pendulum swings back and forth. Freedoms get instituted, and then they get undone and redone. As we know, legislative change doesn't necessarily derive from or guarantee communal change. The social landscape always feels volatile. But with this election, there's a different degree of waking up to what has, for many, been latent—and to the brutal history of the US. That history just keeps fertilizing the present, including aggressively oppressive currents.

SB Yeah, and if Hillary were elected it would not have erased sexism or racism. I remember when Bush Jr. was president and Donald Rumsfeld was secretary of defense. Rumsfeld was giving a speech, and he was breaking down language about the knowns and the unknowns. It was like abstract poetry or just breaking down language till it was nonsensical. Some of the tactics that Trump uses are related. He's using very general language like *great* and *awesome* and *amazing*. It's going to be *unbelievable*, things like that.

JA Right, which it is.

SB It's empty and not really saying anything. There's this nonsense aspect to it where it's very hard to argue against it because you can't be rational and win. There's an absurdity that feels terrifying. It's also in the package of this bully figure.

JA The bully-figure potential dictator—all the more frightening for being so outwardly irrational.

SB Defiantly.

JA I think there's a danger in anchoring *Shared Eye* to the election in the representation of the work, even though you made it in that set of conditions. The narratives of this election and what Trump epitomize are so dramatic. *Shared Eye* has a longer life beyond it being of a moment, no matter how complicated that moment is. Structural, formal, and methodological issues can get overshadowed. And cosmic issues are brought to bear in the suite as a whole and the way that you've created it in the Renaissance Society.

SB In *Shared Eye* I was drawn to making something that had a structural device, of working within the mathematics and structuring template of Blinky Palermo's *to the people of N.Y.C.* [p. 141] I wanted the trace or outline of something that was there and not there. I wanted to think about how the election highlighted the past because you are supposedly evaluating each candidate for their history, and then the present is also important because someone will win and citizens literally show up on a particular day and vote, and then finally our future is also at stake, so it's this magnified moment where the chronology of time gets compressed. I was interested in working with the structure of a loop during this moment—when you walk into the space and see the show, you see that it's larger than you can take in. You can see what's in front of you and what's behind you, but you can't see everything or anything unless you hone in—get up close. And all the parts kind of build up.

Conceptually, I wanted to have this trace of another work—a kind of ghost. I wanted to work with images that were more photographic but in a subtle way still referenced painting.

JA When did you decide to adopt the framework of *to the people of N.Y.C.*? Was it something that you'd been thinking about for a while, something that was buried in a sketchbook?

SB Yeah. I had been thinking about it before the Renaissance show became a possibility. I was partly thinking about *to the people of N.Y.C.* because I had spent a lot of time looking at it. It had a big effect on me. And I also had been thinking about miniatures and working with small panels that were about head size.

And I kept having these memories of when I saw Palermo's piece at Dia, where at the beginning of the piece there were seventeen small panels like six inches tall, grouped in sequences of threes and fours. They feel cognitive. They're at head level. I decided to make a few panels that were that size, and work with objects and images that were very small.

My mom collected all these knickknacks and tiny objects in the house that I grew up in. The keepsakes had emotional value or were familiar. When my grandfather died, he had saved this small shoebox that had his driver's license and a few little knickknacky things in there. I'm like, "This is what he saved?" That is what he wanted to have preserved.

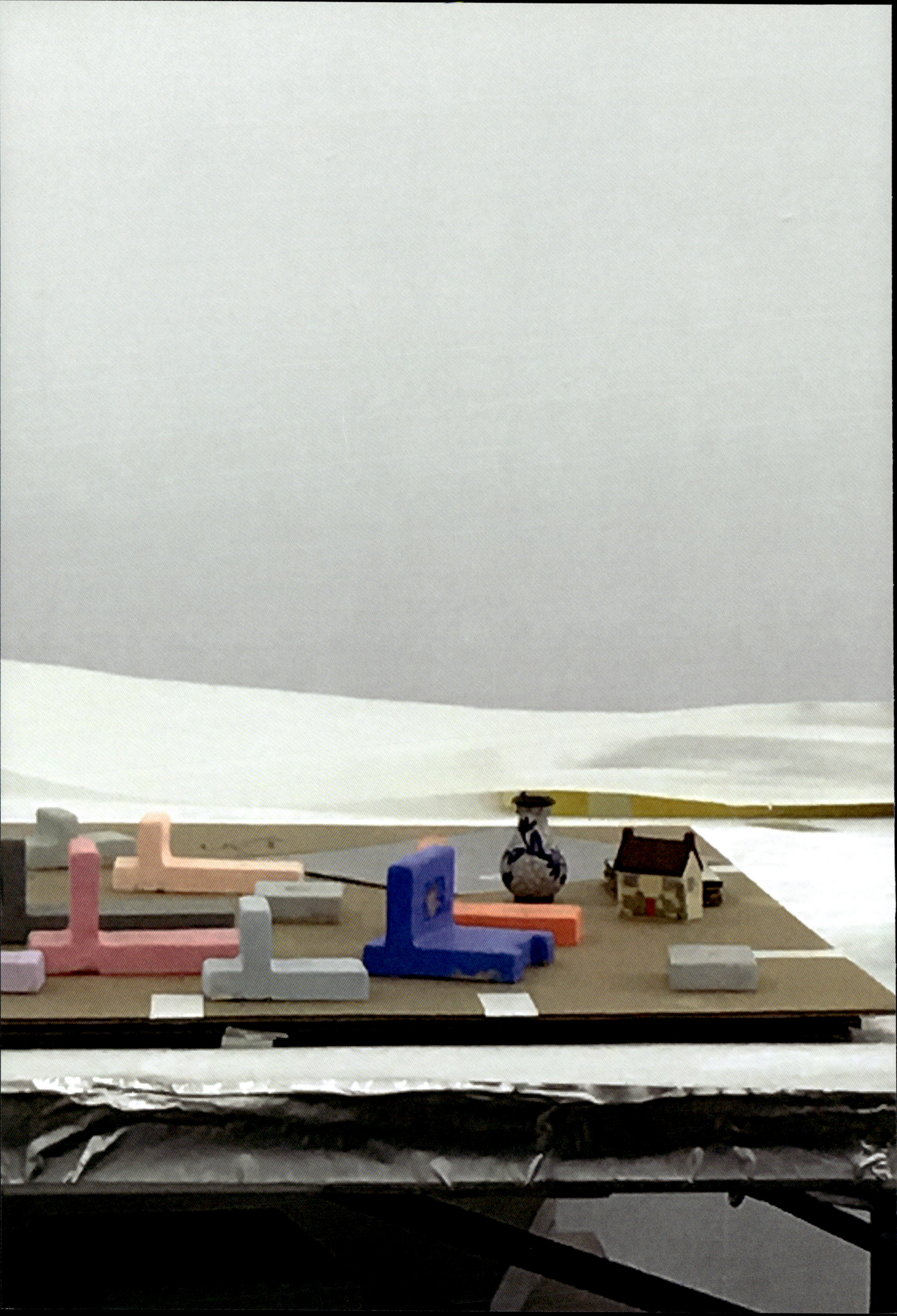

I guess the content and the ways in which the photography also functions in the piece are thinking about change and loss, and also the compression of digital and analog photography as coexisting compartmentally in the panels.

I was working with triangles of threes because in a lot of the Palermo panels there are three bands of red, black, and yellow. I wanted to have symbolic relationships to some of the elements that were in Palermo's work, but also not. They could be musical improvisations in a way. They didn't have to be obvious. Working within the template made the work change. The way I would frame a digital photograph when I shot it had different frame ratios from the dimensions of Blinky Palermo math. I liked that it made me reframe my original images—it tightened the frame, and I ended up feeling that the digital images that are in the work had a different effect when they were cropped. They're honed in; you're a little closer, even though you're kind of off and far away from things. And there's a physical feel to that. It's like zooming in while driving in a car backward at the same time—there is a physical effect.

JA There are practical reasons for adopting Palermo's framework, and you're indirectly joining to his work and the spirit of the title, *to the people of N.Y.C.*. Do you feel or intuit a particular affinity with Palermo the artist and person?

SB Often when I work on something, there's an element that feels potentially awkward or scary or like failure is around the corner. There's fear involved in how to relate to something. What do I have to say about this—especially if the person is well known? It also felt like an interesting challenge to understand what it would be like or what would happen if I did.

Palermo died before the piece was shown. I don't know how it might have been had the artist been alive to install it. So the work itself has a dimension of translation. In terms of affinity, there are a couple of things. The surfaces of his work feel really human. They have a humane sense of touch or something. The quality of the paint and the way the panels are thin and open on the back—they have an air of gentleness.

I can't know anything about the person or his personal intentions; it's the work itself that speaks to me—I like the fragility of it. On some level, it feels like it could be mass-produced, too, because Palermo often used house paint and aluminum panels, which have an industrial aesthetic, but it's the tension between the handmade and the mechanical that I like.

One of the things I thought a lot about in looking at *to the people of N.Y.C.* was that it goes from these small, vertical, head-size panels of threes and fours to a split single panel to rectangular groups of four, then larger horizontal panels that are more peripheral and evoke landscape size. So there's this scale shift back and forth throughout the work that was very important to me.

Having to morph yourself in and out of different-scaled realities is a real day-to-day human experience. Like how the economy works, understanding the difference between a dollar and a trillion dollars or something; we have to imagine these impossible scale shifts. And also our daily experiences with technology and moving between all these different-size screens and virtual spaces. More and more, our experience requires having to project a lot, project into spaces that are much smaller and much larger. So the scale of *Shared Eye* shifting back and forth, and also between singular and plural sequences, is important to the content of the work.

JA I like your example of conceptualizing the relation between a dollar and trillions or the national debt. On a simple level, I think of the scale shift from head size to billboard size as akin to personal and public. The elements in the project combine to become panels, and the panels combine to become groups. The groups combine to become a whole. I imagine you holding these different scales in mind simultaneously while making the work. Analogously to an understanding of oneself as multiple things, as an individual but also a compilation, an idiosyncratic compilation. Also oneself as a group constituent, how we identify with lots of associations or possible groups. And then as a member of the larger collective wherever one wants to draw that boundary, whether the collective is a small circle or family or tribe or about citizenship or humanity or life-form. The *Shared Eye*, e-y-e, is also a shared "I." The notion of "I" as a compilation of histories.

Within the structure, there's the collaboration with Palermo and the accidental collaborations with internet sellers, who may or may not be the original makers or owners of what they're selling. In my experience, collaboration is usually intimate and risky.

SB I don't feel comfortable with thinking about the found objects as collaboration because I question how that might function. The original story of how I started working with the found photographs was that I had a memory of a photograph that I took when I was a kid when I was with my dad at the zoo in Milwaukee. And my dad used to have it at his house in New York City. It was a photograph of a zebra. My dad had a fire, and he lost his home. I believe that the zebra photo burned, too.

I decided to search for "zebra, photograph, zoo" on eBay, and I found a photograph that looked identical. I started to have other memories of things that I don't have photos of, times in my life, things that happened, different people whom you don't have documentation of. And I started looking for images that reminded me of those things. In the process, I found incredible images. It reminded me again of this shoebox that my grandfather had with a few things that mattered to him, and how things end up being not with the people who originally took them.

There's a rescanned fragment from *Citizen Kane* in one of the panels in *Shared Eye*, a black-and-white close-up of a bunch of junk—packages and boxes. At the end of *Citizen Kane*, when all of Kane's stuff is being catalogued, and much of it is being preserved, and some things are being discarded or burned—there seems to be an economy for what is saved or what becomes disposable. I looked at the photos that I had started collecting as being things that I didn't want to be lost. Each photo as a representation of someone's life, some time or place that seemed important.

I was interested also in the unknown of that—I didn't want to work with photos where I knew who the people were. I wanted to have an unknown within it. I wanted to deal with perception and its relationship to identity, and I wanted to also highlight the humanity of the people in these pictures. This is part of why I inserted a shelf with keepsakes, the three-dimensional object that comes out like a portal from the photograph as an offering with an aura—to see an object that is so obviously an object, I think, makes it harder to objectify the people in the photographs and heightens their reality.

JA The images create lots of points of entry without becoming defined handles. I think *collaboration* was the wrong term, not just because of your reaction. It's funny. I know *found object* is a term in art, but I wasn't thinking of the images and miniatures you included in that way. I regarded them as models of depiction and documenting. Not that we need to name it, but you've been acting curatorially in the sense of accessing, with particular criteria, the immediacy to everyone and everything that the internet provides as a resource. There's a broad range of moments and perspectives and phenomena that work their way into your piece.

SB Well, maybe they're not found as much as they're located.

JA They're sought.

SB In order to find something you need to have search terms—language is assigned to catalogue or archive. To politically position yourself, you have to give your political ideas or identity words. So, on the one hand, we need to have categories so we can be seen, and, on the other hand, everyone wants to defy the categories because no one can quite fit into any.

I've thought about that in terms of Occupy Wall Street, because people were critical that there was no central focus or leader, that there were too many different voices and therefore it wasn't clear what exactly OWS stood for. But that was what was so important to me about seeing and experiencing the many protests I attended—that I identified with the network and fabric of the diversity, and that the questioning or confusion that might arise because of the diversity was real, but that did not mean OWS lacked in clarity. Like what you were talking about, about how the panels in *Shared Eye* both have individualities and have the group, and that the structure is a loop—which has an open-endedness to it. So there's an infinite way of thinking about the piece. When you look at these images and think about them, you might think differently about them at the beginning than after you've seen something in the middle or elsewhere. Or whatever route you take, because people walk the piece what I might consider backward or skip around and reedit the order, so there isn't necessarily an exact chronology I can enforce.

JA The project got made within the arms of a specific period, and it simultaneously transcends that because all the included artifacts embody clock time, historical time, lived experience, and different registers of relating to time. A modeling of consciousness takes place. And the piece does away with the "arrow of time," which is the way we understand time as linear. Scientists agree that chronology, and the designation of past, present, and future as distinct, is a human perception that was invented to apprehend experience and not a physical fact.

SB There's a mix of time in the kinds of photos that make up the piece. There are snapshots, portraits, photo-booth pictures, and telefaxed images from newspapers. So they have distinctive contexts or purposes. An illustration for a newspaper is trying to depict a given narrative. And when someone is posing for a portrait, they're trying to capture something about themselves, or when somebody's taking a picture of a friend or of family, they're capturing a narrative moment.

My family would use photography as a way to remember things. So your memory of something was from this photograph rather than from what happened. Photographs become this kind of delusional device that alters history. My family would often use photography as a way to construct a given memory. There was a photo my grandmother had on her wall. It was an image of me from a Kmart portrait studio—every Easter she would take me there and dress me in some insane long dress with a bonnet and I would cry all the way there in protest of the misgendering parade we were on, and by the time we took the photograph my face was bright red and traumatized looking. My grandmother loved these photos and often referred to the good time we had that day, which I knew was not true, but it's how she experienced the event.

I saw an amazing Russian photograph of Joseph Stalin in a show at the Met called *Faking It: Manipulated Photography Before Photoshop*. Over time, the image had been altered to paint out or erase three people due to political change and censorship. It's fascinating, with the historical tension between photography and painting, that painting would take revenge on the photograph in this situation or be used to get the document to reflect a manufactured reality.

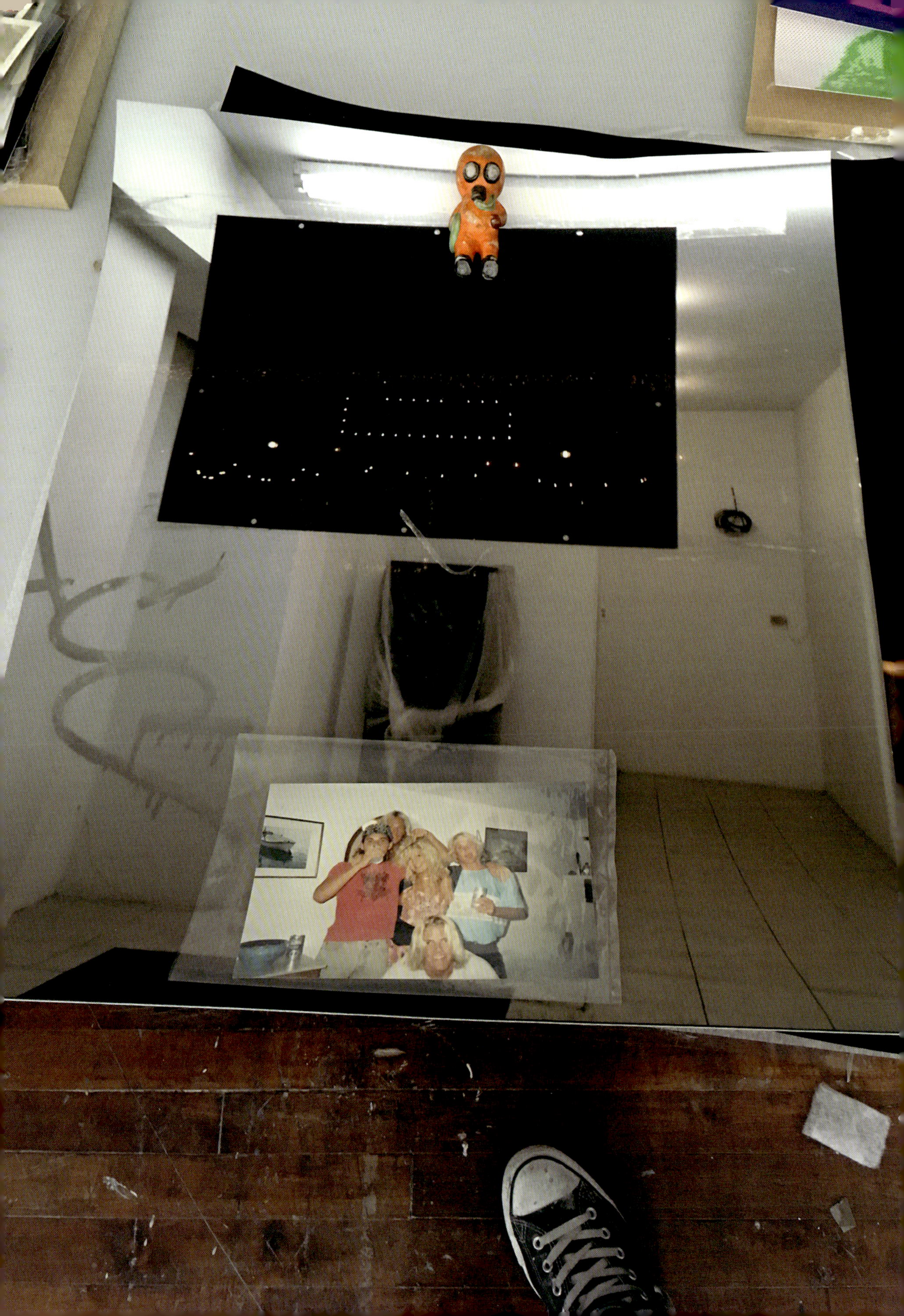

JA More than one psychoanalyst and theoretician has talked about how photography and photographs can obscure actual memory by creating a stand-in that takes the place of the dynamic aspect of memory, which would imagine something past as more present. Some believe that photographs conceal memory rather than deliver it.

SB I think about that regarding language, too. If I think about gender and all of the possibilities each person could manifest about who they are in terms of gender, not just their biology or what they're assigned, but how they feel inside throughout their life from day to day, moment to moment, I feel like each person has a wide range, maybe some less than others, but I think every individual is very much their own gender. But when it comes to the constrictions of a binary language system, we end up with a limited ability to perceive as a consequence.

JA Language is expressive, and it's also oppressive. It prevents as much as enables. You're spot on about time, too, because, of course, time-telling through clock time, as we know it, is an invention of the Industrial Revolution. Calendars from other epochs and cultures work with natural phenomena. But the Industrial Revolution changed the conception and measure of time in Western culture.

SB I don't know about you, but I don't have a lot of memories from my childhood of having conversations with adults—I can't remember any of them. [*Laughs*]

JA Yeah. I can only remember one conversation, where I asked my mother what sex was. I was sitting in the bathtub.

SB I have two conversations I remember. One with my grandfather where it was New Year's Eve, and he was explaining to me why people were celebrating. I was like, "What?" He was trying to explain the clock and the calendar and why we would be celebrating the end of one year. I remember it felt like this very extreme thing to relate to. I learned a lot about math from my grandfather, so I loved talking to him about numbers. But just something about the calendar seemed crazy to me.

And then I remember talking to my mother. She was trying to describe to me what irony was because I saw Andy Kaufman on *David Letterman* and he was doing the wrestling stuff. And it kind of freaked me out, I didn't know if it was real or not. I was like, "Is that real?" And my mom was like, "It's irony." I thought to myself, "These are like deep philosophical matters."

JA That's hilarious, your resistance to understanding clock time and irony. I watched an episode of *Seinfeld* last night where all the characters are stuck on different subway trains. Elaine is stuck on a train, and an older woman starts talking to her and says something like, "Yeah, I remember the old days when men would get up and offer you their seat." They're both standing, and all these guys are sitting in the seats, and Elaine says, "Yeah, it's ironic, we've come so far, but I'd really like to sit down." The woman says, "What do you mean?" And Elaine says, "You know, it's ironic, like, as women we've come so far yet we haven't." The woman says, "No, what does the word *ironic* mean?" Elaine can't explain but has this exaggerated expression of disbelief. It's hilarious.

SB It's a really hard word to explain, actually.

Recorded interview, February 28, 2017

JA It seems to me you effectively achieved an open narrative in *Shared Eye*, and I'm thinking about how that works.

My first glimpse entering the exhibition induced a desire to move near to the works as well as a flash of frustration, because obviously there was no instant content payoff, and that was intriguing and seductive. The installation compels us to dive into the room and move close to the panels and to take in the compositions and relationships as we move around the room with the goal of considering and deciphering the images and associations. I was always alternating between studying the panels and their ingredients and surveying the rest of the room from each stop or vantage point—looking near and far and using both direct vision and peripheral vision.

You need to hold multiple scales in mind and visually while engaging the work to build implications. This is a consequence of how you mapped *Shared Eye* onto the space and staged viewing experience, which seems to be very precise in setting up a field of exhibition narrative without defining that narrative.

SB I wanted to have this feeling that when you walk in you're aware of this timeline that moves around the room, that you actually see the length of it. You see there's more of it than you can grasp at one time. You're going to have to, like you said, see the farness of it but also approach it as something you have to work at individually.

That being a kind of experiential thing that you get from the dimensions of the space, and that's maybe particular to the experience of seeing something that's durational, a moving image, where the frame is moving on top of itself in time in a single frame. There are a lot of reasons why that was an experience I was interested in evoking. I feel like it has a political dynamic to it.

JA What's the political dimension?

SB A lot of the images within the work go between outside and inside, and can be read as external or internal—I think of the political dynamic in terms of interacting with a person or seeing things out in the world and how you're bringing your assumptions to the encounters. The way that you can't necessarily experience all of what an individual is or what an experience is, so there's a spectrum of experience that's happening outside of the event.

Some of this has to do with identity and how the show is thinking about perception—how people project their own histories onto the experience of looking and seeing, which has a politics to it, in some cases violence, since this can result in hatred: racism, sexism, or xenophobia.

JA In the show, we readily cross-connect different scales and images and concepts. It's similar to how, in the current technological environment, you might reflect inwardly and look at your cell phone or iPad, and be surrounded by media and be with and near people—be involved in multiple communications and thought processes all at once. We have the cognitive tools and visual literacy for all of that. What's unusual is to be in such a carefully distilled version of that kind

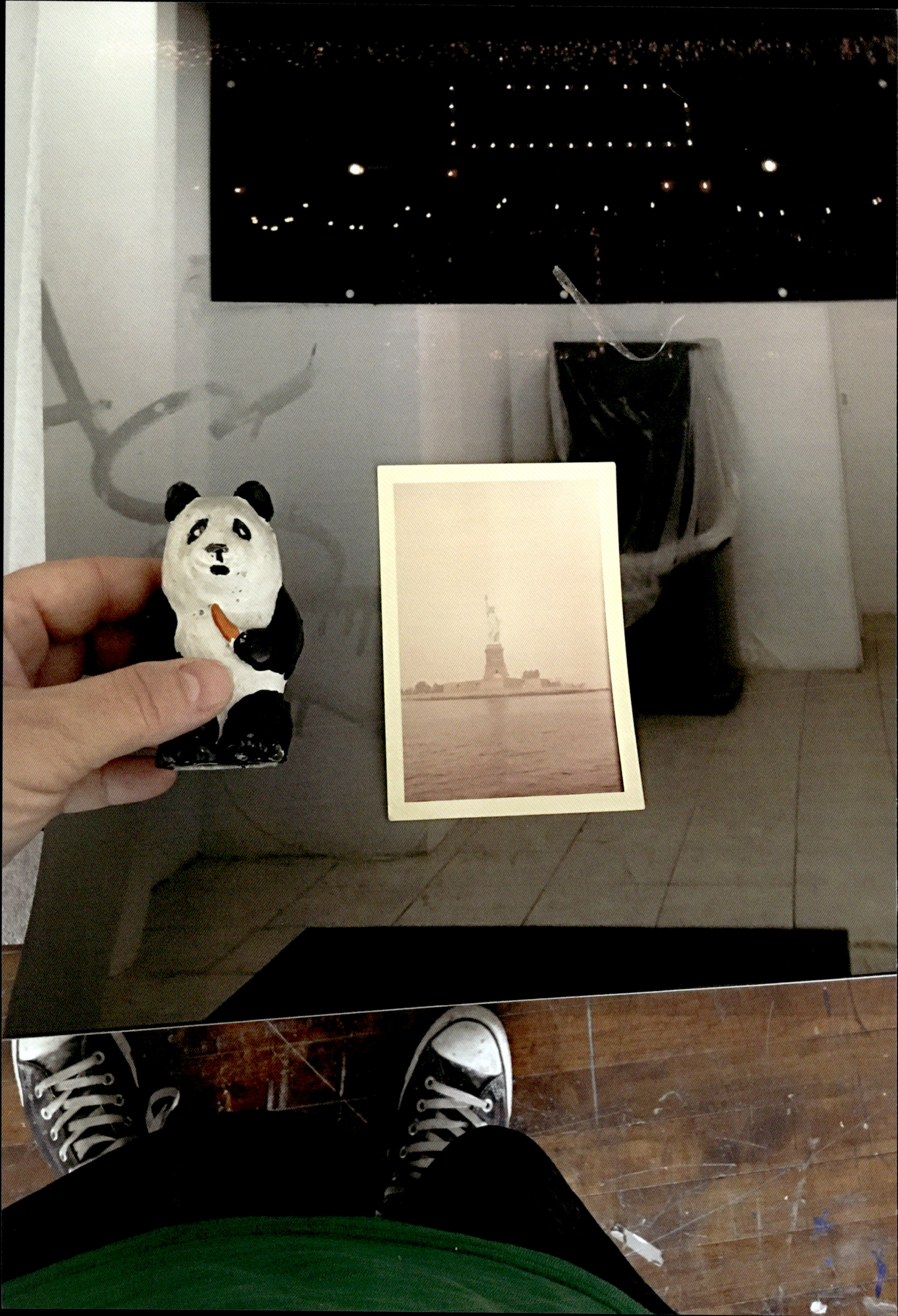

of diversity of information, which the show was, that is also spacious and contemplative by design.

You organize the ingredients, and they accumulate into a whole, or panel, that accrues into another whole—a field of vision. There's this image repertoire that includes snapshots of unrepeatable moments that seem explicit but are at the same time generic and emblematic. These images retain mystery as puzzle pieces that, taken together, don't form a complete picture. *Shared Eye* positions the viewer in a situation where the identity of the protagonist is up for grabs, where we psychically particularize meaning while being in the midst of the installation.

I wonder if scale, and how you think about scale in your work, is always a fragmentary proposition.

SB In part because I have a history of using video, scale was something I was already concerned with. Video can be projected at various sizes or put on a monitor. So it can be in a space that's theatrical and cinematic, or it can evoke a space that's more personal or domestic—like the way we watch media on our phones, or the experience of watching television in our living rooms, kitchens, and bedrooms. Also if it's shown in the darkened space of the cinema, it has this other context of the mind. And the camera can also zoom in on what you are seeing, and editing can recontextualize what you were originally filming.

I remember having this experience of making videos and then screening them, where I was shooting things very close up partly because the camera I used was so low-res that I had to be physically near or the image wouldn't look like anything. It would be too abstract. I would shoot parts of my room, handwriting, objects, photographs, or my face, and then when I projected these things in a theater, it was like my eyeball was 150 feet wide and after the screening during the Q&A when I was standing there I felt like I needed to apologize for being five feet tall and not an actual giant.

It made sense to me that identity would be represented in this fragmental way because there's no way to depict the entirety of what a person is in any one document. Now that I'm working with mediums that are more sculptural, or about drawing or painting, I'm still thinking about fragmentation, but it's spatialized differently, and other types of relationships are possible because the mediums are shifting.

Also it makes me think about the subconscious and that in-between state when you are falling asleep and you're in a dark room with your eyes closed but you still can hear sounds off in the distance—you're not sure exactly what your scale is or where your body ends and the space begins. You're kind of in this other state.

I think shifting between scales in the work, from miniature to large, is asking the viewer to expand their vision in a way that references that subconscious state. I was also influenced by seeing many of the Merce Cunningham Dance Company performances at Dia over several years, which were site-specific events. The audience was encouraged to walk freely around the space of the performance and therefore would have vantage points that were changing. It also meant that you could not actually see everything at once as in a more traditional theater presentation where the audience is seated facing a stage and all the action unfolds frontally. But with the setup for the *Beacon Events*, there were simultaneous performances happening throughout the space and a loss around seeing. We only get to see so much. We don't get to see everything.

JA The experience of the installation at the Renaissance Society is physical and metaphysical at the same time. I had the impression that space was morphing in the viewing process, receding and coming forward and expanding and contracting. That was fascinating because it was physical not only on the scale of my body or my perception in relation to the panels, but the entire space was activated by how you meshed these things in that space.

Maybe scale shifting is a feature of all of your work—that there's a simultaneous activating of personal scale and collective-public scope and larger amorphous dimension, together, all the time. Like, it's not possible to have one without the other.

You said in an interview that there was something musical about shifts in scale and perspective. Is that applicable to this installation?

SB Sound is physical. The way we actually hear sound is that it's moving. It's in space. It's bouncing off of things, and it has a parameter to it that we can move in and out of. The musical also refers or relates to the mathematics of the Blinky Palermo piece, *to the people of N.Y.C.*, because there's a rhythm to the structure of the threes and the fours and the ones. It has a time signature to it in terms of patterning, which has a musical quality.

When I made work that was black-and-white, I thought a lot about color. Not that black and white are not colors, but that there's a range to black and white that reads as different colors. Even though *Shared Eye* is silent, somebody asked me, "If this had a sound track, what would it be?" My answer is that it would be a lot of radios on at the same time, many different channels of different types of noise. There are multiple levels of things happening, so there are images colliding within the same frame. Some of them might be silent, some of them might be quite loud, but they interrelate.

I was also thinking about linearity and nonlinearity. I'm affected by using technology as part of my everyday experience. When I started editing video in 1990, I had to edit in a linear way with two tapes and a controller, and everything got recorded onto a master tape from beginning to end, so you had to go in order.

Later I learned to edit in a nonlinear way using an Avid where I had all these bins with thousands of clips of footage, and I could see this overview of time or have multiple timelines going. I could copy things and move them around. It affects your brain when you're using technology as part of your process. *Shared Eye* has both digital and analog images within it. It also considers a relationship between linearity and nonlinearity. Part of that has to do with it being a loop. Even though I have a route I think is right for me, it doesn't mean someone else has to go in that same movement. I've had an experience of making a video that's on a loop in a museum or gallery; people can walk in, and they're not sure where they're walking in, and they're seeing it out of order.

That experience is also a musical one. I often will listen to one song on a loop and repeat for hours. I like how the song stops having the original order and starts to have an out-of-order experience, because you forget where the beginning is when you hear something over and over again. I was also influenced by making electronic music, sampling and thinking about hip-hop music—how people reorder things, recontextualize cultural material to have a different meaning for them.

JA This circles back to what you were saying about balancing linearity with nonlinearity or a different spatial model within the piece. The panoramic view when you walk in suggests chronology that gets reinforced by an aspect you pointed out to me when I saw the show: the cyclical element implied by the subtle shift from daytime to nighttime in the photographs that you shot, which form the ground for each panel. I probably would have perceived the changing light but not put two and two together to articulate the cycle. The show proposes a kind of itinerary, but it's also antichronology.

SB I was partly thinking of the cycle of the day as a kind of loop, too, because we keep doing it over and over again. This cyclical understanding that we have of time. Even when the work is suggestive of the cycle of a day, the way it unfolds from day/blue sky to night/black sky and back to day/blue sky, I was interested in disrupting the "flow" or read of what depicts these times of the day. So that night isn't always seen as dark—maybe night is a twenty-dollar bill, or because of electricity the frame is blazing with neon—or that daytime is seen in the reflection of a dimly lit store and therefore could really be any time of day. So the chronology of time is there to be seen but not always as you might expect.

JA The cyclical, revolving, looping dimension of the installation provides a sense of movement and of time unfolding as the environment of the work operates or as we perform the work.

Of course, you could enter anywhere, but visitors don't usually walk in and go every which way. The work hugs the walls, so you tend to go to the left or right, and pretty quickly, whichever way you're going, a sense of something cyclical develops. When you're across the room and you look back on the doorway you entered the space through and will exit through as well, it also becomes part of the loop.

In *Bomb* magazine, Lia Gangitano talks about how you scripted the physical space of the show you did at Participant in a very particular way, and you said, "What I like about dealing with an exhibition space is that editing becomes dimensional. Like what's near something else suddenly creates a juxtaposition similar to editing in a video."

I want to know more about your spatial thinking in exhibition form. You seem to develop an installation vision when you're creating a body of work, especially when you pair a set of works with a particular presentational context, like *Shared Eye* with the Renaissance Society. The way you integrate work and exhibition space strikes me as subtle, precise, and intently sensitized to viewers. That vision encourages particular experiences and discourages others. So I don't know if you have something like a philosophy of installation.

SB The work is developed with the space of the exhibition in mind, knowing it's going to be in a specific location. I make work the size it should be for a particular wall.

Initially I conceived the *Shared Eye* work for the Renaissance Society, but I was also thinking about it becoming the core of an exhibition of the same title at Kunsthalle Basel. I specifically made many other individual works to accompany it there.

The Renaissance Society space is so tall and has this huge ceiling; it's like a spaceship with a church inside it. It's not a typical experience. It has a heightened reality to it, which I wanted to contrast by making work that would equally engage with its own sense of logic. It's not necessarily a philosophy, but I learned over time that if you make work that takes the exhibition space into consideration—maybe it's even subtleties like the difference between making a panel fifty-three inches or fifty-one inches—it effects how the viewer might intuit what the work is about and operates on a subconscious as well as physical level, which is important to me.

I was reading about the piece that Blinky Palermo was working on before he died, *to the people of N.Y.C.* The work, as well as diagrams and notes for it, were found in his studio after his death. I was interested in that particular piece, as it was installed without people quite knowing how he would have installed it for himself. In looking at the documentation of the piece, it hasn't been installed that many times, but the few times it has been, it has been installed differently due in part to the architecture of the spaces.

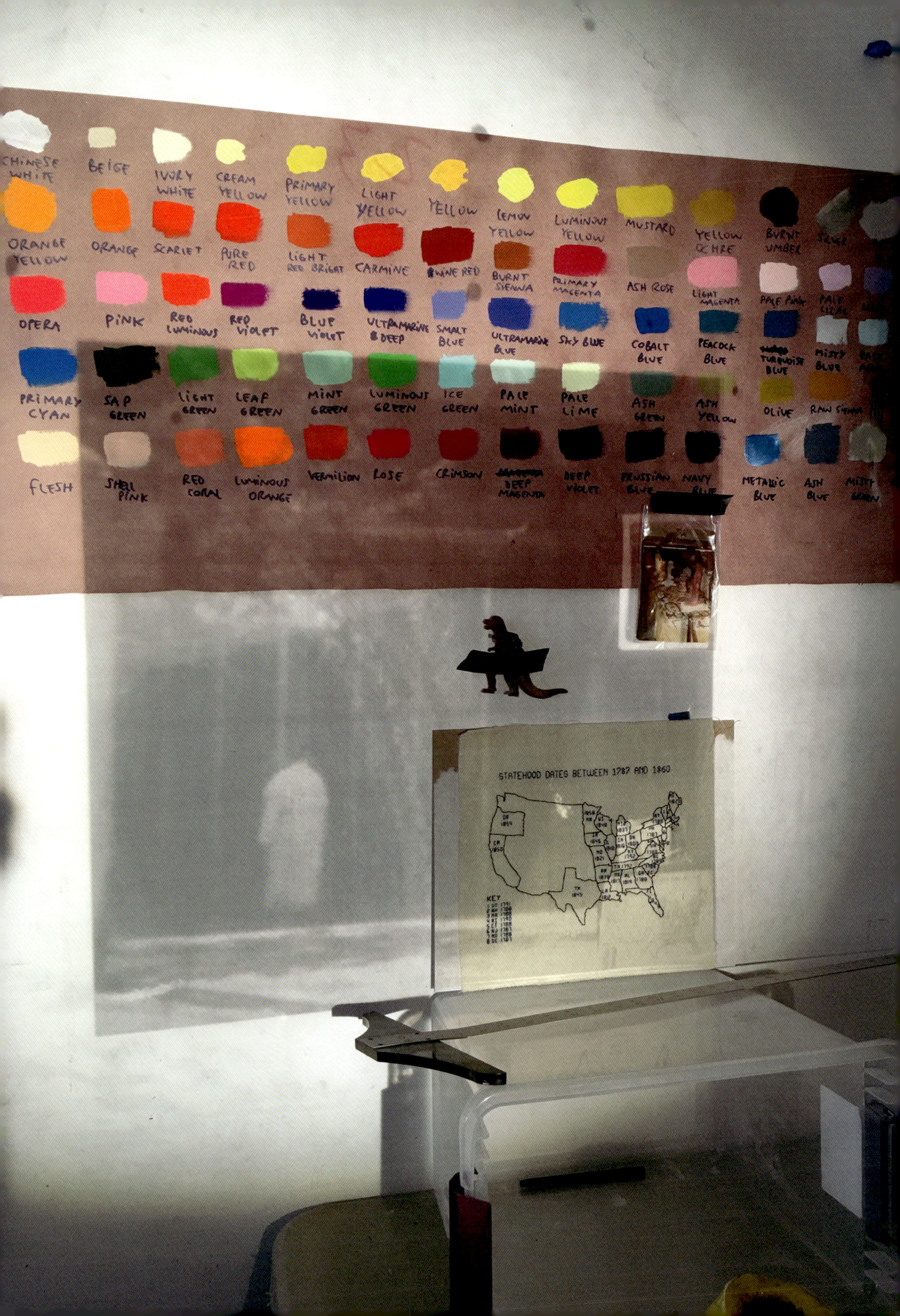
CHINESE WHITE
BEIGE
IVORY WHITE
CREAM YELLOW
PRIMARY YELLOW
LIGHT YELLOW
YELLOW
LEMON YELLOW
LUMINOUS YELLOW
MUSTARD
YELLOW OCHRE
BURNT UMBER
SILVER
ORANGE YELLOW
ORANGE
SCARLET
PURE RED
LIGHT RED BRIGHT
CARMINE
WINE RED
BURNT SIENNA
PRIMARY MAGENTA
ASH ROSE
LIGHT MAGENTA
PALE PINK
PALE LILAC
OPERA
PINK
RED LUMINOUS
RED VIOLET
BLUE VIOLET
ULTRAMARINE DEEP
SMALT BLUE
ULTRAMARINE BLUE
SKY BLUE
COBALT BLUE
PEACOCK BLUE
TURQUOISE BLUE
MISTY BLUE
PRIMARY CYAN
SAP GREEN
LIGHT GREEN
LEAF GREEN
MINT GREEN
LUMINOUS GREEN
ICE GREEN
PALE MINT
PALE LIME
ASH GREEN
ASH YELLOW
OLIVE
RAW SIENNA
FLESH
SHELL PINK
RED CORAL
LUMINOUS ORANGE
VERMILION
ROSE
CRIMSON
DEEP MAGENTA
DEEP VIOLET
PRUSSIAN BLUE
NAVY BLUE
METALLIC BLUE
ASH BLUE
MISTY GREEN
STATEHOOD DATES BETWEEN 1787 AND 1860

JA Installation is a dynamic part of your practice. You don't make a fixed installation plan for a body of work or just plug the work into a space built to order. You had the opportunity to re-experience installing *Shared Eye* at Kunsthalle Basel recently, and with other ingredients. What did that installation involve? What did it change or open up in the work?

SB While I was generating *Shared Eye*, I knew that it would travel to Kunsthalle Basel, so I made the work also with this relationship in mind.

In the Kunsthalle, the space splits the *Shared Eye* loop in galleries four and five with a wall and two doorways, so instead of the loop being in one room, it's continued into two. When you look through the doorway you can see that it repeats and keeps going. You walk through galleries one, two and three to get to galleries four and five, where the *Shared Eye* loop is. You then go through galleries four and five and have to walk back through galleries one, two, and three in order to exit. So in Basel the *Shared Eye* loop isn't the only loop—it's a loop inside a loop. It's kind of infinite, like a mirror looking at a mirror, but not so trippy—it's more about the experience of walking, like how when you hike on a trail where you hike in and then have to turn around and hike out on the same trail you walked in on, the way you see things on the way back is always so different from the way you saw them on the way in—your perspective has been flipped.

So when I installed in Basel I was dealing with how you might leave things out so there is a reorientation that happens upon entering gallery one, where there isn't an image on the facing wall or on the right. Everything is very linear and on the left. You have to turn your entire body and orientate yourself to each individual image, and galleries two and three also continue this kind of favoring to one side. The extremity of this kind of hanging exacerbated the turnaround effect because all the work switches from left to right when you have to walk back past it upon exiting. So in one direction when you enter rooms one, two, and three, it looks like there might not be any works on the wall until you turn the corner. I wanted a feeling of things being missing or off register, and then when you come back through the work is now on the right side and is the first thing you see or is more apparent.

In Basel, for the additional work, each panel is its own frame ratio. There is no sequencing of successive panels of the same size. If I think about it in a more musical way, you have a prologue like with classical music where you have very different types of time signatures or structures—which feel like introductions. In this situation you actually have to exit or "end" by going past the introduction or "beginning." But I wanted you to feel like, when you walk into gallery one, it seems like you're in the middle of something. I wanted you to loop around and be back at the middle again rather than the beginning or the end. I didn't want it to feel as though, "Oh, you're starting here." I wanted you to walk in and go, like, "What is going on?" which is more what you would be like if you walked into the middle of a Hollywood film. You're like, "What the hell is happening?"

I learned something from my grandmother because my grandmother had Alzheimer's, and I remember going with my father and my grandmother to see *Rain Man*. So you're watching this narrative film with somebody who can't remember what happened. Every scene is like a brand-new story. She'd be like, "Why is he driving a car?" The narrative logic made no sense to her. I was probably thirteen or something, but it made me realize not everyone has the same way of understanding something.

JA That's pretty good. And *Rain Man* no less.

SB That really stuck with me.

JA The Renaissance Society is one room, so you're aware of the whole when you enter. Did the installation in Basel have a placeless feeling?

SB What I tried to set up wasn't placeless but rather more pedestrian. So it is about urban space. I don't know where a lot of the found images come from. They come from many places. Those are more mysterious to me, but most of the photographs I took were taken in New York City, where I live, and were gathered over several years. I walk everywhere, so that sense of being a pedestrian was something I was thinking a lot about, and that also relates to the video I made with Solveig Nelson called *Play Pause*, which is about transitory states.

At the time I was living between several cities and constantly traveling. I was waiting a lot. I was on trains or planes, or in between places. Specifically, I was thinking about the importance of those kinds of places that are public where you're together, and in a way you have anonymity there. And thinking more intensely about that after September eleventh just because of anxiety around terrorism and what that resulted in—

JA The war on terror.

SB —invading Afghanistan and Iraq, and the response to 9/11—it being used in such a fucked-up way is disturbing. Part of feeling free or being in a democracy is that you want to be able to walk down the street and not fear that you're going to be killed or blown up. But on some level, growing up queer, and growing up, as a child, female, and growing up in a neighborhood where most of my friends and community were not white, I was aware of the fear of being killed, and these things happening anyway.

JA The pedestrian aspect is fascinating. It's funny, I think of urban space more and more as placelessness or a place of displacement. In my experiences of *Shared Eye* as well as *Play Pause*, I had the sense of being located and placeless at the same time.

I'm glad you mentioned *Play Pause*, because there are a lot of points of contact between it and *Shared Eye*. They are both epic works that weave together narrative fragments and cultural symbols, and personal and collective and public moments, and glimpses into lived experiences. In *Play Pause*, there is a structured stream of images and ideas, and in *Shared Eye*, there's a surround, but both works seem epic, and both are taking the cultural temperature. In the case of *Shared Eye*, you're checking America's feverish temperature.

There's a lot of transiting and transition as subject and mode in *Play Pause*, and a kind of spirit that feels lost or saturated by losses—things are on the verge of obsolescence. *Play Pause* and *Shared Eye* both invoke urbanity. There's so much that is on the brink of obsolescence and passing from the present in these evocations of the city.

There were more motions toward a utopia in *Play Pause*, if I think of the sexuality in it as utopian. I don't know if there's an idealistic proposition in *Shared Eye*. Maybe that dimension is located in your methods at work?

SB In order to even approach utopia, change and introspection are needed. So I wouldn't necessarily say that *Shared Eye* isn't concerned with those things, but yes, it's not so much depicting idealistic representations of a utopian world, although I find the humanity in the images to have a utopian effect or quality, and especially in Basel in gallery two—*Fia* and *Garden* I would point to as works that are generative about hope and desire.

JA You mentioned that *Play Pause* was in part keyed into or came out of the attack on the World Trade Center—and how the ground shifted with the political directions taken afterward. You talked about the keying of *Shared Eye* to the 2016 presidential election, and the uncertainty the campaigns unleashed. Your early videos were informed by the AIDS crisis and your engagement with ACT UP in a particularly formative period for your thinking and working.

September eleventh and the war on terror, the 2016 election, and the first-wave AIDS crisis can all be understood as paradigm shifts—personal and collective paradigm shifts. I'm wondering about the relations between sociopolitical transformations and your methodological pivots. Some methods, media, and forms you were working with coalesced in *Play Pause*, and as far as I know, it's the only larger piece like that in your work over time. *Shared Eye* also embodies a coalescence of different media and modes you were beginning to work with but hadn't brought together in the way you did for *Shared Eye*.

SB When there's a paradigm shift, often there is obsolescence embedded in that reality. So there's usually something that is traumatic about it. I think when you're making work, and you're responding to things that are happening around you, there's an intense amount of unknown. When I was a teenager, and I was first coming to terms with being queer, and so many people—friends and family—were dying and dealing with HIV and AIDS, it was an urgent time. You wanted to respond in whatever way you could, whether it was political or creating some type of resource to creatively cope with it. So being inventive was an important mechanism.

I do think of art as being a part of having a life force while you're here. And one of the things I'm very aware of is that there are a lot of queer artists who are no longer here because they died. I guess as a queer teenager it felt that much more imperative to spend my time wisely.

JA That's very cogent. In both *Play Pause* and *Shared Eye*, retrieval comes into play as a modality. You're vivifying and rescuing what is almost history. There's a similar impulse to retrieve in *Shared Eye*.

SB There's that, and also a desire to forge a combination of elements to make a visual language that's understandable in a new way, because I feel that language is often not good enough. It's obsolete as well—the boxes we check for race, or ways of categorizing gender that don't make sense to me.

That comes from an intuitive place—wanting to develop another way of speaking, and some of that has to do with not being understood or protected culturally, where bathrooms are segregated by male and female genders, and regularly I am policed because of this, told I don't belong or asked to leave. It affects your brain and your ways of seeing and thinking about things.

JA And they shape society. Language discourages indeterminacy, and one of the things that render *Shared Eye* so potent, and that is initially disconcerting, is the absence of narration or a narrator. By design you're not telling us "This is what I think," or "This is what you should or may think." We know the body of work has been authored or organized by someone, but there's no overarching narration, and we fill in the meaning. You've refrained from any declaration of signification, but the piece itself bespeaks an atmosphere and climate. It's speaking but also defying language and its capacity to freeze content. That seems very useful.

Irresolution is in the foreground and on the surface, in the constellation of artifacts and the whole they configure. Spending time with the work I started thinking about my ability, as well as our collective capacity, to tolerate ambiguity, and for how long. Usually, in exhibitions, we're coddled, given handles and signage and reductive declarative text, which together can prevent fresh experiences. Here, you've made a space for me, the viewer, and you invite every viewer into that conceptually open space.

SB There have been times when I have made work where I felt like I needed to explain things, or needed to create a voice-over. Times when I thought I was being very clear and knew exactly what I wanted to say, and even then I didn't always see something that was glaringly obvious to the audience. There's always this meld of your consciousness and your subconsciousness working in tandem. Then also the audience is going to be having that split consciousness going on when they are having a visual experience. I'm interested in this murky place where ambiguity exists—it's psychological, but it can also be material, like how things are put together, where you're not sure what exactly the material is—they look like photographs, but I would call them paintings. It's that confusion or tension about what something is that is central to my work.

JA You've spoken about using a building-up approach for *Shared Eye*. The panels bring different elements together without leveling them, or doing so in a seamless way that I imagine would be alienating. You've physically embedded elements within other objects or larger panels, which renders the photos more tactile. The seams and sutures are a prominent aspect of the panels. The effect intensifies the bodily relation with viewers. That isn't a model of cut-and-paste graphic space, but one of implanting things within one another.

SB I like how mediums can retain their independence even when they are dropped into a new relation to one another. I'm not trying to erase something about one particular medium when I juxtapose them.

In the way in which the photographs were handled, I did not want to treat them as this kind of delicate material that you could ruin or something. I wanted to work with them as tactile parts of the piece. It's still a photograph, but it's sanded, shaped, and cut, which pushes its fragility or indexical quality—as made evident by its marks and crinkles.

I was thinking too about newspapers and the way the paper is folded with distinct columns and compartments for language and frames of photographs that illustrate the stories—a newspaper has its own structural logic, which I thought about when working with the images in *Shared Eye*.

JA The analogy also comes across in how disparate pieces of information and economies get seamlessly configured—when a news story is next to some advertisement placed above an entirely different news narrative, and another ad, etc.

Maybe the newspaper format with its conventions of headlines and storylines is an example of the violence of language that short-circuits intricacy. The newspaper is hierarchical, and I think you also avoided hierarchizing the diversity of material you included. You've avoided the perils of language in the work.

SB I was thinking about the structure of a newspaper as a container more than as a literal thing—how there are many frames within a frame. For years I would paint on top of newspapers, as a kind of template. Which also reminds me of making electronic music using an Akai MPC2000—where you're working within the constructs of a given set of parameters that you fill in with material and then make sequences that you gather into lists in order to create "songs."

JA One thing we haven't talked about is how we have to improvise the piece and free-associate while within it. When I encountered *Shared Eye*, it felt like a dreamlike collage that takes up the whole room, and the room is collage—there is a dream-space quality to these things that are floating in and out of view. Part of the effectiveness and generosity of the work is that it makes that opportunity in the space of an exhibition, in contrast to a media space or a city intersection or in one's own dreams. I don't know if you've read Freud's *The Interpretation of Dreams*.

SB Yeah, I sat in on Laura Kipnis's class at Northwestern. It was amazing.

JA I got a lot out of her book *Against Love: A Polemic*. I read *The Interpretation of Dreams* when I was in Sweden for a four-month residency. I sent myself a giant box of books there that I needed for both research and leisure reading, and the books never arrived. So I went to the nearby art-academy library, which had a lot of English language books, but I didn't especially want to read art books. I noticed that they had an edition of the complete works of Sigmund Freud. So I decided to read all of Freud and consider it both my thought-provoking reading and my recreational reading. I didn't allow myself to take notes. I wanted just to read. Reading Freud like it was fiction or something was fantastic. And *The Interpretation of Dreams* was especially engrossing and illuminating.

SB In the class I took with Kipnis, we would read it, but we were supposed to utilize what we were discussing in class and what we were reading from this text within our own creative lives. This involved paying attention to our dreams and writing descriptions of these things; then we were supposed to collectively exchange these and work on something that wasn't our own with someone else.

JA With *Shared Eye*, each viewer navigates the terrain independently using particular social, personal, and psychic filters.

SB I like thinking about the improvisation of the viewer, because that's something collage can aid in. Collage doesn't necessarily need to be an improvised experience when you make it. But something about the format creates a shifting associative ground that feels improvisational to look at. I do think spacing out is important. When I've listened to a lot of live music, experimental jazz, especially when I lived in Chicago, at the Velvet Lounge or Hot House with artists like Fred Anderson, Roscoe Mitchell, Tomeka Reid, and David Boykin performing—part what was so incredible about the experience was the effect it had on the brain. Listening expands the mind.

When I was beginning to learn about jazz, I went to see Sun Ra in high school, but I didn't know how to listen. I liked the music, but I had been conditioned to hear in constricted ways. Sometimes in the process of listening to jazz over the years, when there is a buildup of noise and hearing musical distinctions becomes more and more difficult because all the players are going at once, as a listener I feel my brain drifting, clearing out the junk it contains, and then at some point a melody or hook will pull me back and I'm there again.

That's another version of scale shifting because you're here and then you're also somewhere else. It's very much like a pedestrian experience when you're walking down the street and you're looking at the world around you but you're also in your mind thinking. This kind of simultaneity feels like how we experience life.

JA This internal reflection and external stimulation come together in *Shared Eye*. One thing about free-associative terrain or free association and improvisation as modes that seem productive is that when I'm in the work activating it, and it's activating me, that's a unique experience. It's not repeatable. The next time I'm there I'm going to be sparked by different thoughts or images, memory or connections. The project is a template for experience and is also a production site for unique experiences, for independent thinking.

SB From having made videos and dealt with the world of cinematic programming and the people who go to the movies or want to see experimental video art, in that process of developing as an artist and as a person, I was taught to think a lot about an audience and what they're bringing to the experience. I physically would be there to talk to the audience for years every time I showed my videos. So it was like the opposite of putting something on YouTube, because I had to carry the tape to the place and be there physically, and there was very little anonymity when you had to be face-to-face.

From that origin, I'm aware that audiences are unique, each one, each person. When I was younger I wanted to cultivate relationships with people through art so I could have conversations, and sometimes I didn't find people I could talk to, not every time. It's rare to find people whom you relate to. The other amazing thing that can happen is, you have this idea of what you want to translate to people, you make something, and then somehow they see it, and someone gets it. And you can become more and more abstract and more and more complicated with it, and people still pick up on what you're doing. It's not necessarily psychic, but it feels like you're transferring something between people. They're attuned to something you are attuned to. It's a pretty magical thing, actually, when that happens.

Installation images

The Renaissance Society

November 19, 2016–January 22, 2017

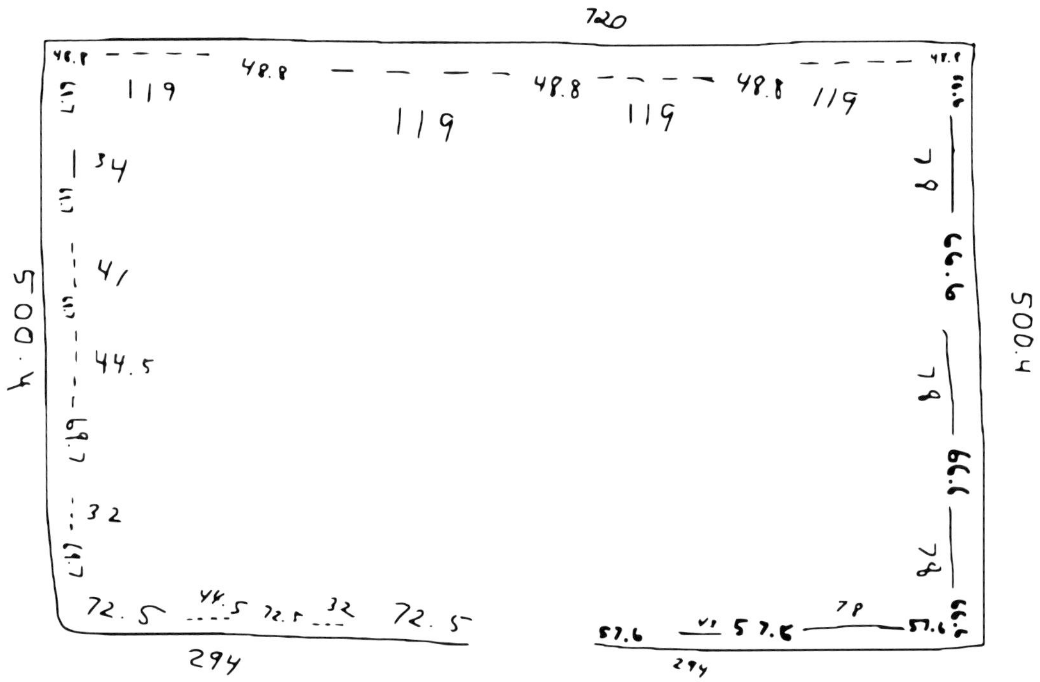

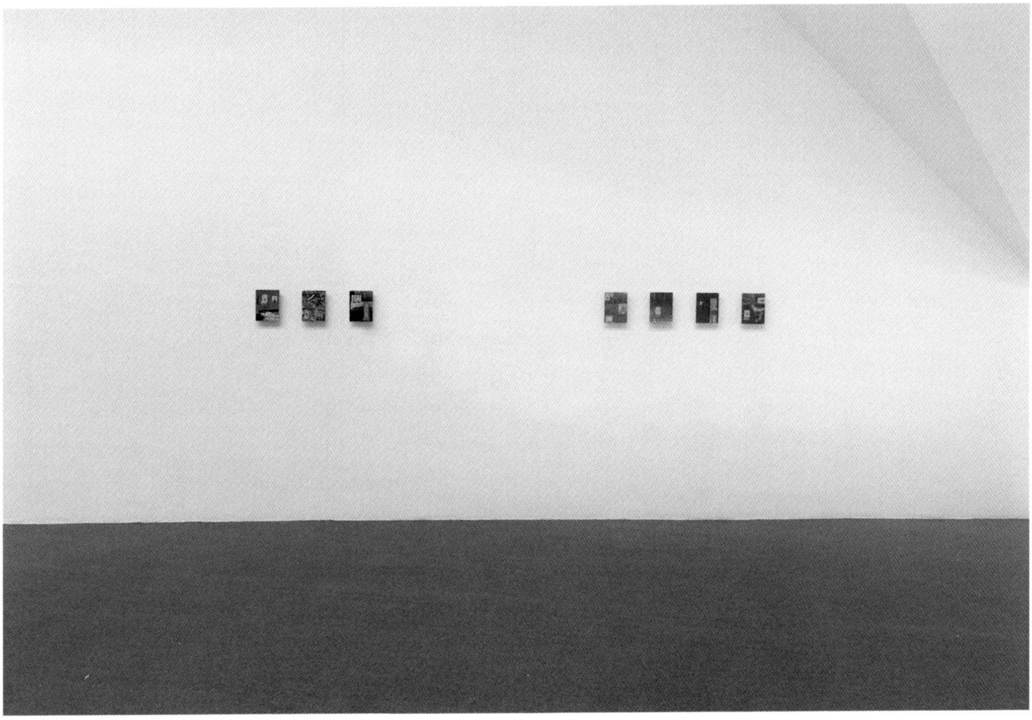

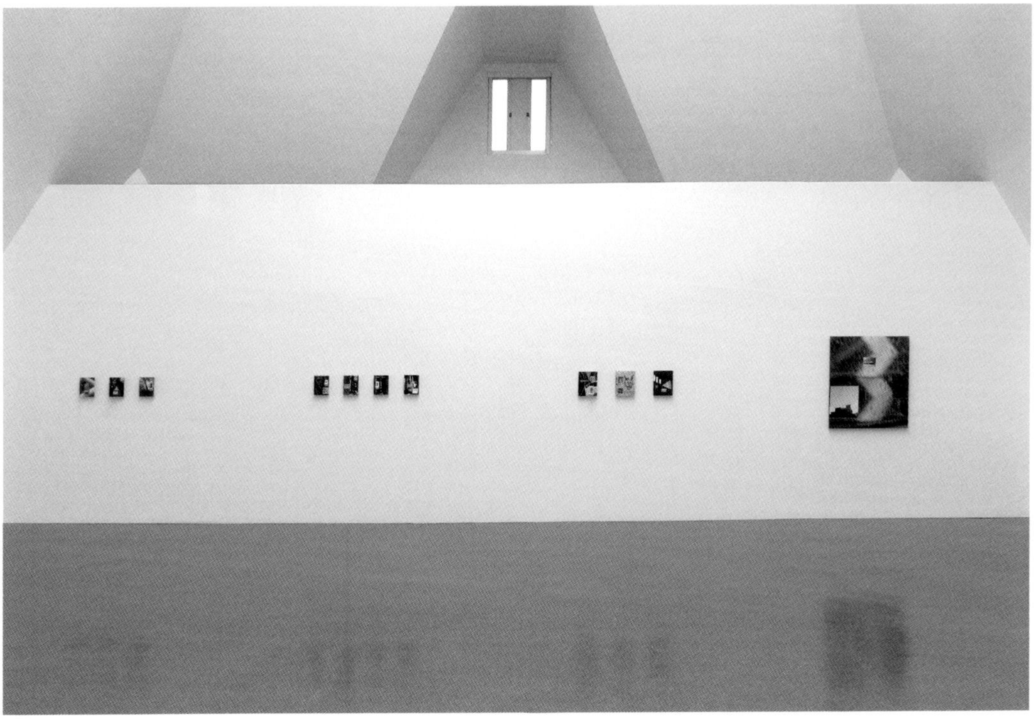

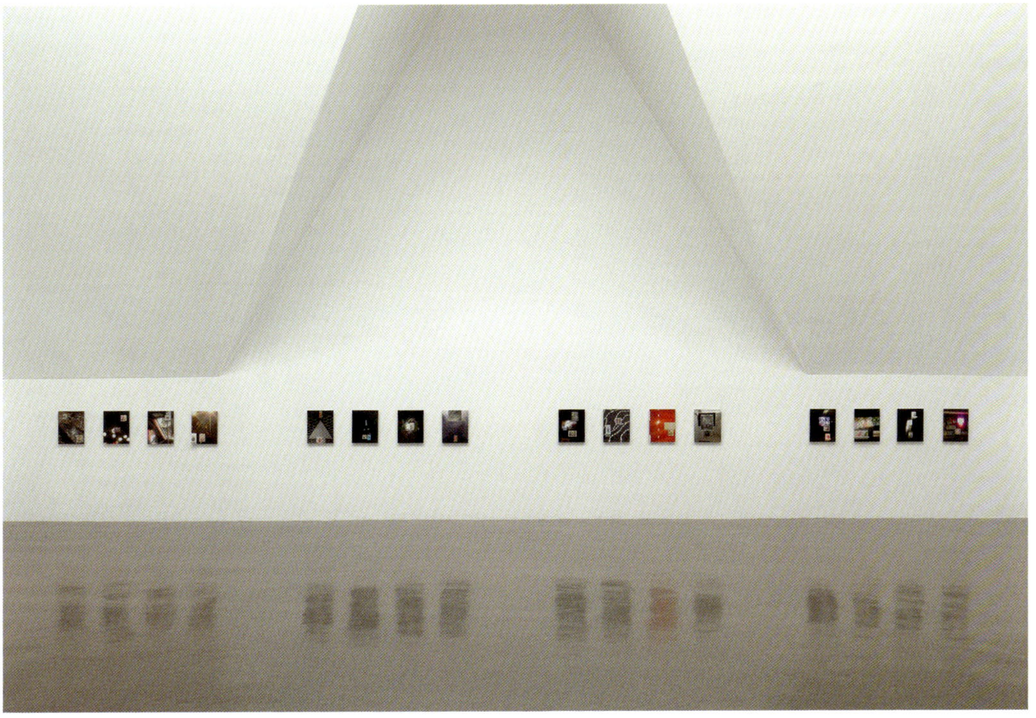

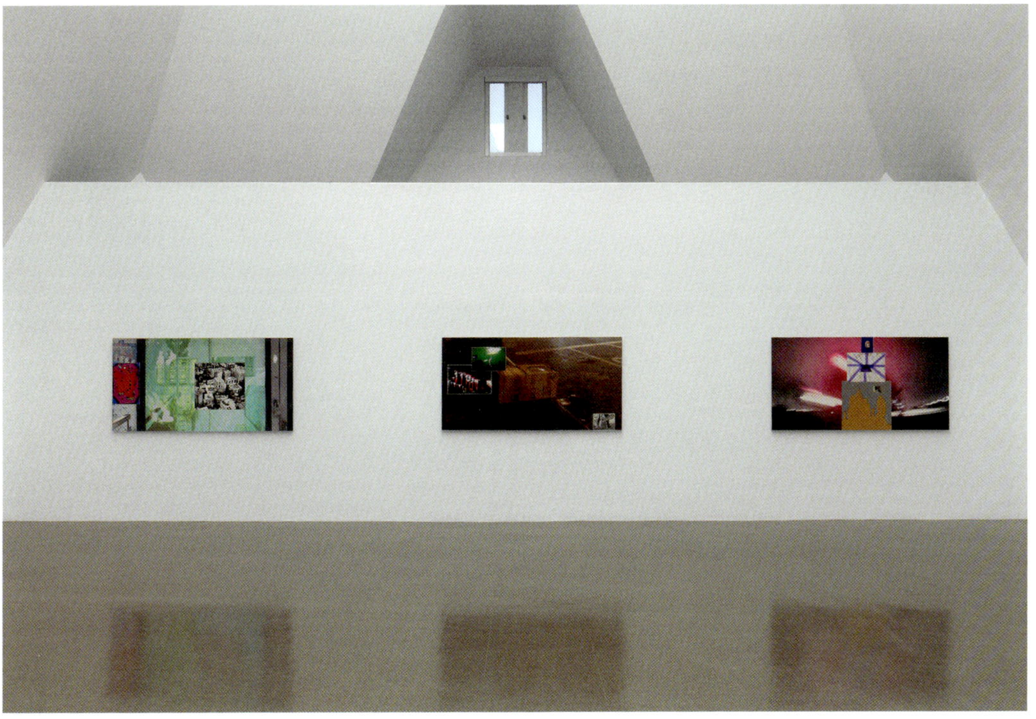

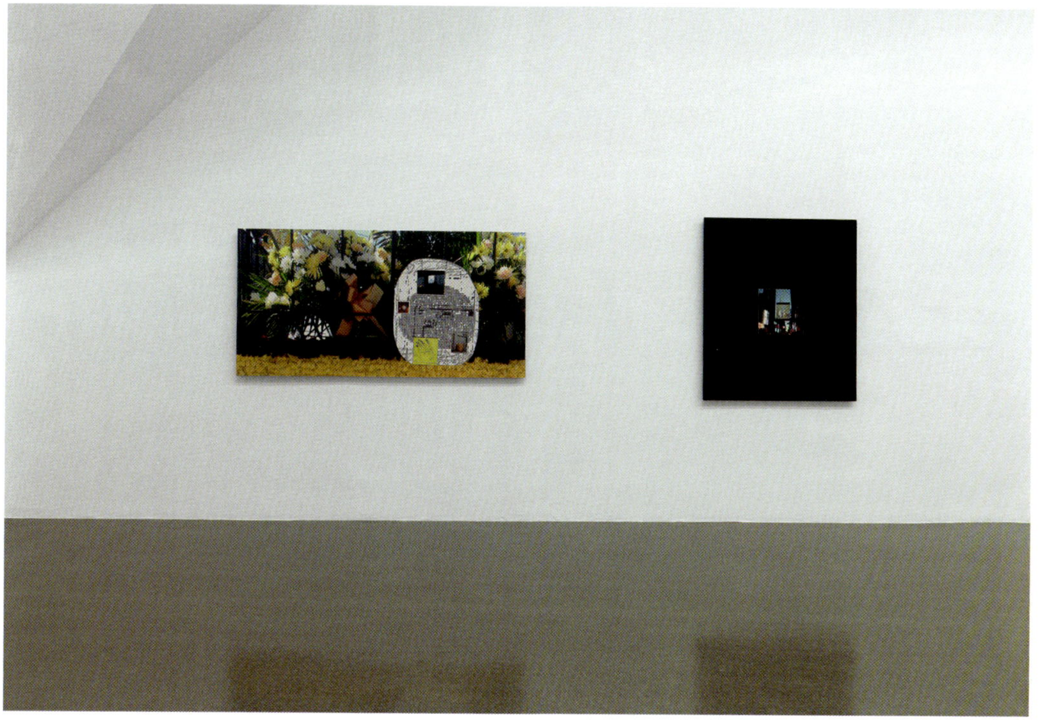

Benning through Palermo's Eyes

Christine Mehring

Forty panels exactly. A room-spanning arrangement of three sets of three, six sets of four, and six singles, in alternations and spacings evidently considered. The smallest panel measuring 21 by 16 cm, the next size up 26.5 by 21 cm, the largest 100 by 200 cm, the concluding one 125 by 110 cm, precisely. All hovering at about an inch from the wall. This description applies to Sadie Benning's *Shared Eye* (2016) as it does to Blinky Palermo's *to the people of N.Y.C.* [Fig. 1] created forty years prior. As striking as these shared dimensions and arrangements appear, all similarities seem to cease right there. Benning's collages of digital photographs mounted on wood and dotted with found analog photos and miniature objects could not be further from Palermo's abstract paintings on metal, featuring mostly variations of horizontal bands that frame monochrome fields in a restrained palette of yellow, red, and black. One an American artist whose signature work with a Pixelvision toy video camera in the late 1980s pressed for nuance amidst the era's omnipresent identity-focused video practices, the other a German whose persistent practice of abstract painting into the 1970s went against the grain of conceptual art, performance, and other new media like video. One emerged as central to contemporary queer art practices, the other firmly rooted in the history of abstraction. A "shared eye"?

Benning conspicuously zooms in and crops the pixilated digital photographs, insets the found photographs, and places tiny objects and figures on relief shelves to step out of the picture, as if to underscore that images, people, and things reign in *Shared Eye*, that human vision desires and fixates on representations of ourselves and our world. Palermo, by contrast, saw and seized the world through emphatically abstract forms, colors, materials, and structures.

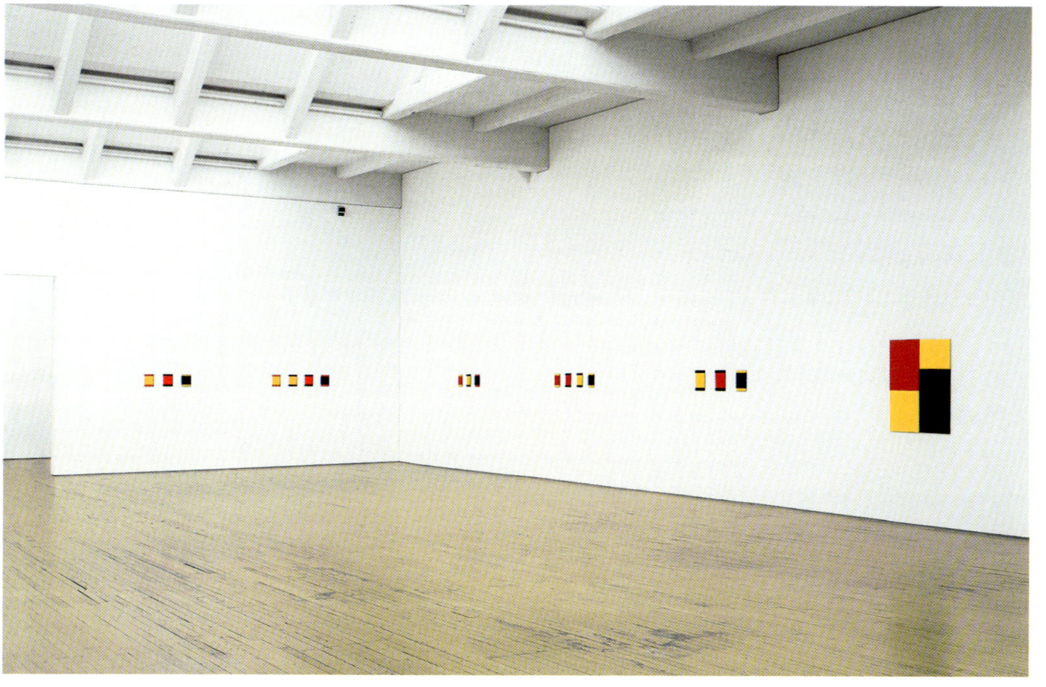

Fig. 1

And yet some details of *Shared Eye*, along with its assertive title, suggest we look beyond superficial stylistic appearances and tired distinctions between abstraction and figuration, painting and collage. There are subtle nods to Palermo's *to the people of N.Y.C.*: remnants of top and bottom bands (a lit-up strip of leopard pattern in panel 5 and a yellow paper garland in panel 38), occasional expanses of color (a radiant ultramarine in panel 17 and an incandescent orange in panel 29), and supple surfaces with subtle sheen and texture (extraordinary especially in the black expanse of panel 40). Rather than "shared eyes" literally seeing the same thing, the title's phrasing drives at a shared way of seeing, even a form of old-style connoisseurship discerning artistic quality and meaning through visual instinct and acuity. From there unravels a formidable intensity of one artist's engagement with the art of another, one that reveals dimensions in Benning's work that have remained in the shadow of the importance of Benning's engagements with video and gender.

As it happened, Benning created the exhibition *Shared Eye* for the Renaissance Society during the Clinton/Trump presidential race in 2016. Reflecting on that convergence, the artist talked about the acute political polarization of the country in the face of impending change, producing intense debate and anxiety, along with a sense of compression of past, present, and future.[1] Complementing general references to passing time—a miniature clock and a calendar, for example [panels 3 and 4]— the images and objects in *Shared Eye* collapse a striking range of historic moments from the 19th century to the present, with the largest share drawing on the postwar period that interests the artist because it shaped the 1970s and 1980s when Benning grew up.[2]

1

Sadie Benning in a conversation with the author, November 17, 2017.

2

Ibid.

Pulsing through these images and objects are the hotly debated themes of that summer and fall of 2016: American identity, difference, and immigration; wars and nuclear threat; power, women, and gender identities. *Shared Eye* takes artistic stock of all that the "United States of America" encompasses and might mean. By extension, the viewer's experience of *Shared Eye* has political implications. Benning's iconographies may be dizzying but insist on a "shared eye," insist on our attempts, that may succeed or fail, to discern allusive relationships between visual fragments and to forge connections across temporal gaps and cultural differences. We alternate between states of productive openness and unsettling uncertainty that the work produces but also mirrors back at us: iconographically in the empty frames of an abandoned sign [panel 12], in precariously tipping race cars [panels 18|19], and in a closed lock paired with the phrase "Let's find out" [panel 37]; or perceptually in obscured views into the distance [panel 5], blinding lights [panel 8], and unidentifiable blow ups [panel 38]. Furthering these states phenomenologically, our experience of the work requires walking back and forth, and negotiating between different perspectives and irreconcilable scales. The cropped details and miniature figures call for close looking, shutting on and off peripheral vision. By contrast, the overall sequencing, spread across an expansive space for which the work was conceived, asks us to stand back, leaving us seeing merely colors puncturing white walls. That peripatetic experience of walking back and forth, close up and away and close again, is figured in select panel pairings, too, as in the shift from an aerial photograph of Manhattan to a painted close-up of light flares in the adjacent panel [panels 20 and 21].

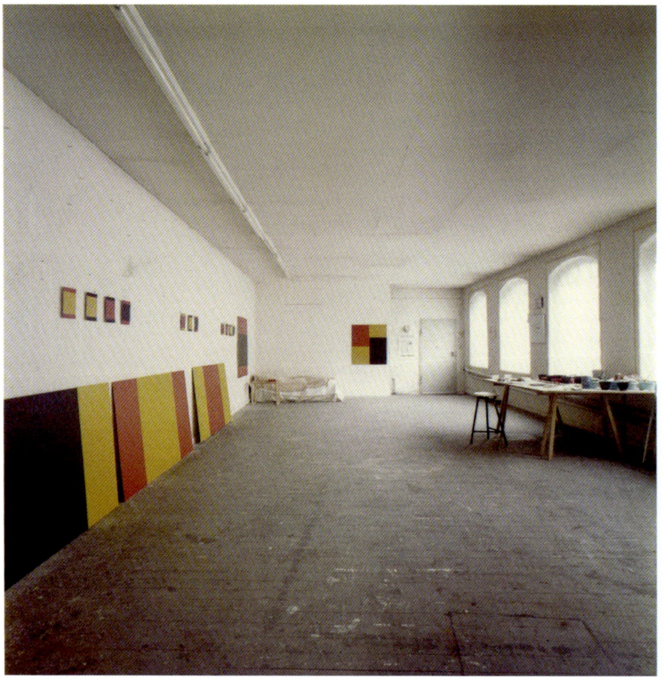

Fig. 2

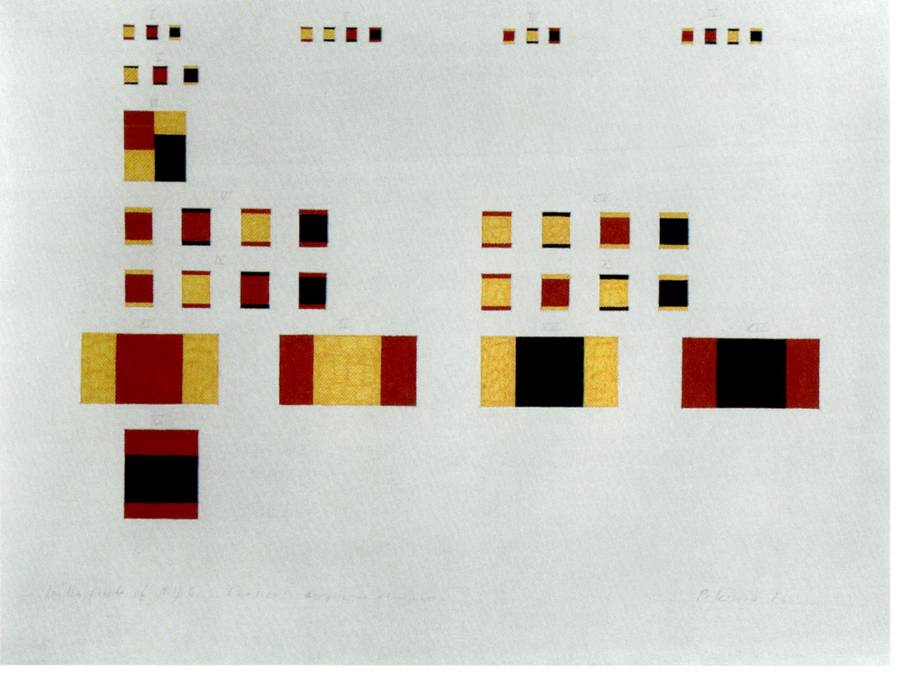

Fig. 3

New York City, where Benning lives, is featured throughout *Shared Eye*. These images present iconographic pointers to Palermo's *to the people of N.Y.C.*, which unmistakably paid homage to the city the German artist had loved and lived in from late 1973 to early 1976. However, Benning engages with Palermo's art not on iconographic but on hermeneutic terms: with the type of meaning his art posits (a historically and culturally invested one), with the thrust of his art's meaning (openness along with the uncertainty that often accompanies it), and with the way his art produces that meaning (through structures, forms, colors, and medium). *Shared Eye* seizes Palermo's "abstraction of an era," which arose from the artist's transformation of dead-ended modernist painting into a historically resonant abstraction that reflected such issues as the postwar economic miracle, the expansion of the contemporary art market, debates about art and politics, and, in the so-called metal pictures culminating in *to the people of N.Y.C.*, an increasingly international art world. [3]

Palermo had created *to the people of N.Y.C.* shortly after returning to Germany after his extended stay in the United States, and its panels were found partially installed in the artist's studio at the time of his untimely death in 1977 [Fig. 2], inadvertently inscribing into this work's foundation a sense of open-endedness and ambiguity that fascinated Benning, among other things: [4] Was it finished? How was it to be installed? Was the sequence outlined in a schematic drawing also found in his studio [Fig. 3] definitive? Might Palermo have reconfigured or otherwise changed what Robert Storr has called the artist's magnum opus had he returned to his studio? [5] In fact, *to the people of N.Y.C.* combines specifically German misunderstandings of contemporaneous American abstraction such as Minimalism and

3
Compare Christine Mehring, *Blinky Palermo: Abstraction of an Era* (New Haven: Yale University Press, 2008).

4
Benning in a conversation with the author, op. cit.

5
Robert Storr, "Beuys' Boys," *Art in America* 76 (March 1988): 167.

color-field painting, reduced to formal and material clichés such as metal, seriality, large scale, and incorporations of real space and viewers, with playful allusions to a system that does not exist—Palermo's recurring yet limited combinations of specific features suggest yet ultimately fail to produce a rationale. The resulting enigmatic artwork was a cultural outsider's answer to a discursive overload in the wake of a heyday of American art writing by the likes of Clement Greenberg and Donald Judd. It was a creative optimist's effort to break open the resulting artistic deadlock so an artist could once again make a move that was not readily categorized. [6] It was also a European artist's attempt to open up the geographic borders of the art world and to put other continents back on the map after New York, as Serge Guilbaut famously put it, had stolen the idea of modern art. [7]

To the people of N.Y.C. and *Shared Eye* each take on historical moments—Palermo an internationalizing art world, Benning the state of American culture and politics. While many artists share such historical sensibilities, Palermo and Benning not only mobilize the same pictorial formats, but make closely related choices about form, structure, and media to insist on a dialectical mindset, even a bodily comportment, of receptivity and doubt. These were highly relevant, much needed in fact, whether in the self-centered New York art world of the 1970s or in the politically polarized American society of the new millennium.

The suggestion yet absence of an organizing system motivates these choices, starting with the shared composition's sequencing and sizes. These have just the right balance of repetition and alternation to make us intuit a mathematical or other type of logic without in the end following one. If Palermo suggested a system more specifically

6

Compare Mehring, "Metal Pictures, 1973–1977: Playing with American Art," in idem, *Blinky Palermo: Abstraction of an Era*, op. cit., 137–171.

7

Serge Guilbaut, *How New York Stole the Idea of Modern Art* (Chicago: University of Chicago Press, 1983).

through the limited palette, horizontal bands connecting across panels, and the consistent placement of a black field to the right of each grouping, Benning does so through a rhythm of recurring colored shelves holding small objects and inset found photographs, and through understated formal devices that connect panels in a given sequence, for example, the arc of white marks and shapes crossing panels 15, 16, and 17.

Before seeing *to the people of N.Y.C.* installed at Dia Beacon in 2011, Benning first encountered some of Palermo's earlier paintings on metal from the *Times of the Day* series [Fig. 4]. [8] In those six works, even more so than in *to the people of N.Y.C.*, unfolding time functions not only as a figure of continuity and change, but also as an agent for taking on different perspectives. The six parts of the *Times of the Day* series, as I have argued elsewhere, work through shifting points of view resulting from traveling between different time zones; Benning creates the same effect by juxtaposing different times of day, different technological eras (analog and digital), different degrees of photographic proximity, from close-up to aerial shot, and different angles on a given subject—a dominance of straight on shots is often pierced by angled one, as in, for example, panels 12, 21, and 33.

For Palermo, nothing was more central to art than color, and it has become increasingly central for Benning, too. For both artists, color prompts an open, if at times unsure, eye and mind. Palermo's palette was simultaneously steeped in vernacular references and insistent on artistic autonomy: the trio of red, yellow, and black in *to the people of N.Y.C.* collapsed the German national colors with Native American color schemes he had studied, suggesting cultural specificity and relativity in synch with their itinerant creator. Other metal pictures showcased colors and color combinations that

8

Sadie Benning in email to the author, March 6, 2017.

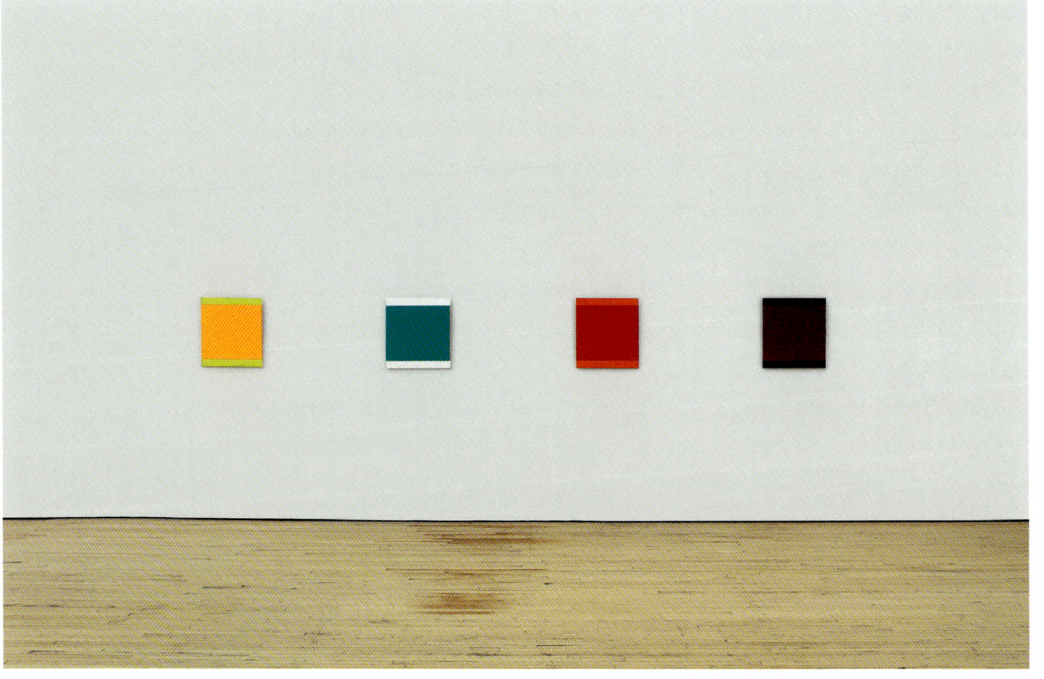

Fig. 4

conjured particular places, like Coney Island, to some, but always felt emphatically idiosyncratic.

In *Shared Eye*, color functions similarly: worldly and ordinary, but independent and artistic at the same time. Benning places blue as a stable unmistakable referent for the sky in panel 1 alongside a different shade of blue reflected off of glass fragments with no clear origin in panel 2. This move is collapsed within a single panel—17—featuring a portion of sky seen through a fence set into a brilliant ultramarine painted surface. Benning opens up gradations in the culturally-loaded color pink by shifting within one triptych from a magenta shelf to a clashing beige on the plastic Truman figurine's suit, both in panel 8, to the pale pink shelf in panel 10. Benning also transforms areas in the photographs that conventionally read as overexposures, light flares, time-induced fadings, or other forms of mishaps into colors perceived largely formally, as, for example, the orange in panel 29.

Following the early Pixelvision videos, Benning has increasingly worked at the intersection of painting, drawing, and digital media. Starting in 2013, Benning developed the hybrid form used in *Shared Eye*, combining found photographs, digital images, and toys or other miniature objects. The digital images are pierced by brightly painted shelves installed in relief, and monochrome expanses of acrylic gouache applied to sculpted aqua resin parts. [9] Crucially, photographic areas, both analog and digital, reveal themselves as emphatically material, like paintings—the occasional crease in the photographic paper mounted on wood, and photographs routinely inserted like puzzle pieces into reserved areas in the wooden panels with visible seams. In turn, painted areas read as elusive, like photographic surfaces; the gouache on aqua resin has a subtle sheen like matte photo paper.

9 Ibid.

Benning, like Palermo, responds to the discourse of medium specificity that dominated American art criticism into the 1970s. "I wanted to deal with my own unease about the separateness of medium specificity. The invention of photography was something that was literally a threat to painting as a medium, and it feels unnerving to me somehow to insert one into the other—like a bad idea, or like sitting the wrong people next to one another at dinner. But I like challenging myself to solve a problem and to deal with the uncomfortable." The flipside of that discomfort and uncertainty is experimentation and openness. As Benning notes, "the history of painting is heavy with arguments, and as much as I am interested in knowing about them conceptually, I don't want to feel oppressed in the studio. I want to be free to try things that don't make sense yet. I put materials together that maybe shouldn't be and don't follow hierarchies."[10]

And in that, we could not be closer once again to Palermo, even though his abstraction of an era did not start from a position of media hybridity like Benning's, but instead broke open stale and increasingly constrained notions of what specifically painting, as a medium, could be: He made so-called cloth pictures sewn from commercially dyed fabrics without using any paint; decorative wall-paintings that perceptually altered spaces and almost disappeared in them; metal pictures made by applying acrylic not to canvas but to smooth aluminum panels that placed the brush lines into relief as the panels themselves hung in relief at a distance from the wall. Palermo intervened into an artistic situation that, one might say, reflected a political one, for the art world's move at mid-century from Paris to New York was part and parcel of a new, Cold War world order.

10

Sadie Benning in interview with Diane Solway, "Transgender Artist Sadie Benning is not Afraid," *W Magazine*, 11 May 2016, http://www.wmagazine.com/story/sadie-benning-artist-mary-boone-callicoon-fine-arts, accessed February 26, 2017.

Fig. 5

Top: Blinky Palermo, *Untitled*, from the portfolio *4 Prototypen* (4 Prototypes), 1970.

Fig. 6

Bottom: Josiah McElheny, *Two Grey Disks after a Prototype by Blinky Palermo*, 2011.

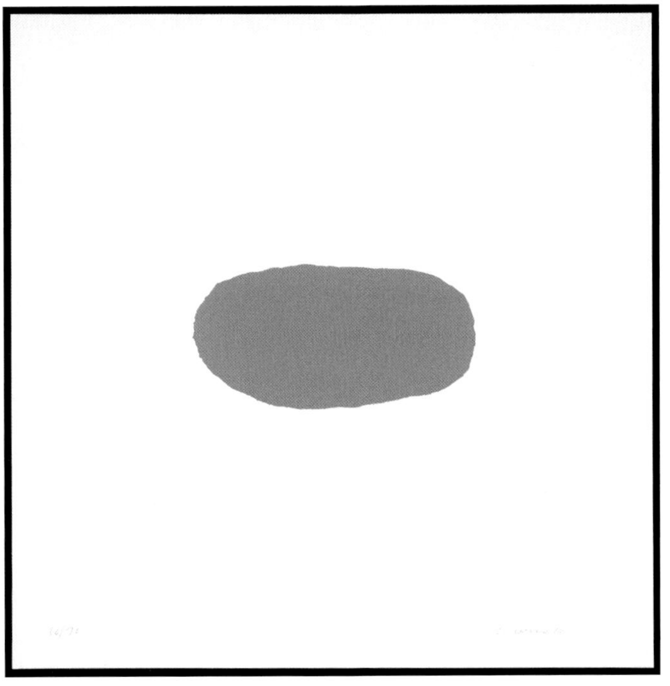

Fig. 5

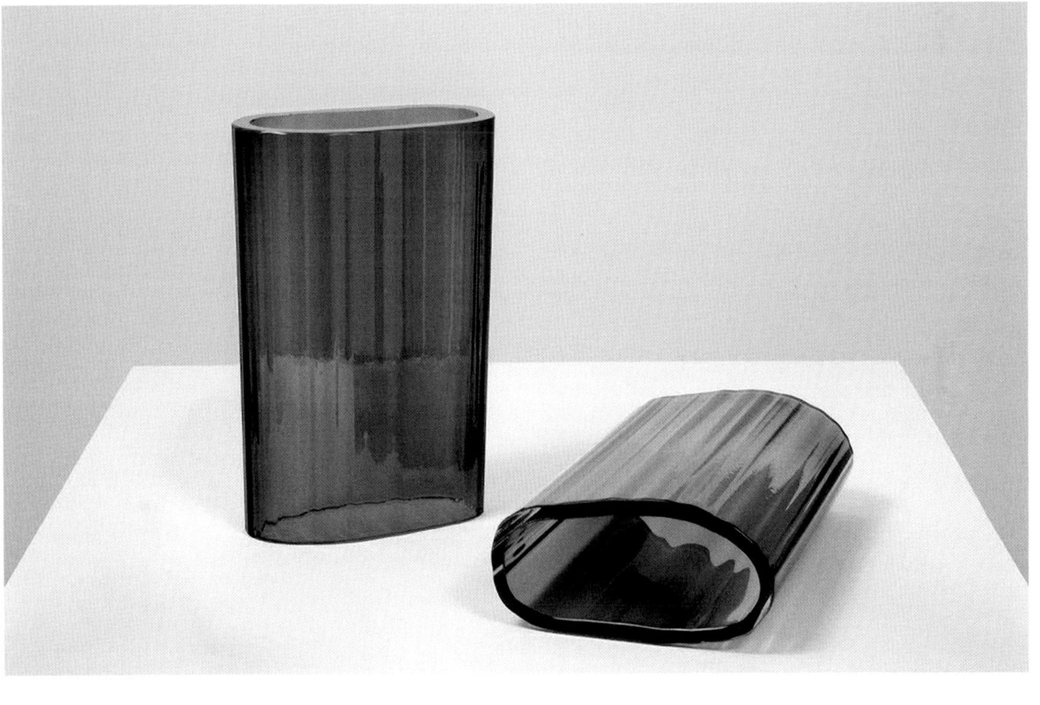

Fig. 6

Like Palermo, Benning is not one to succumb to a naive consideration of art as direct political intervention, but rather is tackling cultural ambitions in the form of artistic ambitions. "People often look at the surfaces of my work and have trouble knowing what exactly it is. Is it leather, is it ceramic? Is it a sculpture or a drawing or a painting...? I'm into that unknown aspect or material ambiguity and see it as having a political context."[11]

11 Ibid.

Blinky Palermo was long described as an artist's artist, in part for carving out creative space for what one might describe as, following Benning, the "unknown aspect" or "material ambiguity" of painting. Indeed, Benning is not the first artist to turn to Palermo. His peer and onetime collaborator Gerhard Richter relied on the younger artist's freedom at moments of crisis in his early career. A very eclectic group of artists, ranging from David Reed and Julian Schnabel to Rirkrit Tiravanija and Josiah McElheny, followed Richter in his admiration and attest to Palermo's openness indeed [Figs. 5 and 6]. With Palermo no longer merely an artist's artist but instead a staple in an art history rewritten in recent decades to include postwar Europe, the imperative in considering such turns to Palermo can no longer be to determine the grounds for other artists' approval of his work. The task instead becomes to reveal unexpected dimensions in the work that draw another generation of Palermo's admirers. As such, those forty panels of *Shared Eye*, in all their identical sequencing and sizing, become but frames to see Benning's art, beyond Pixelvision and queerness, through Palermo's eye: as a vital intervention in the history and contemporary practice of abstract painting.

Installation images

Kunsthalle Basel

February 10–April 30, 2017

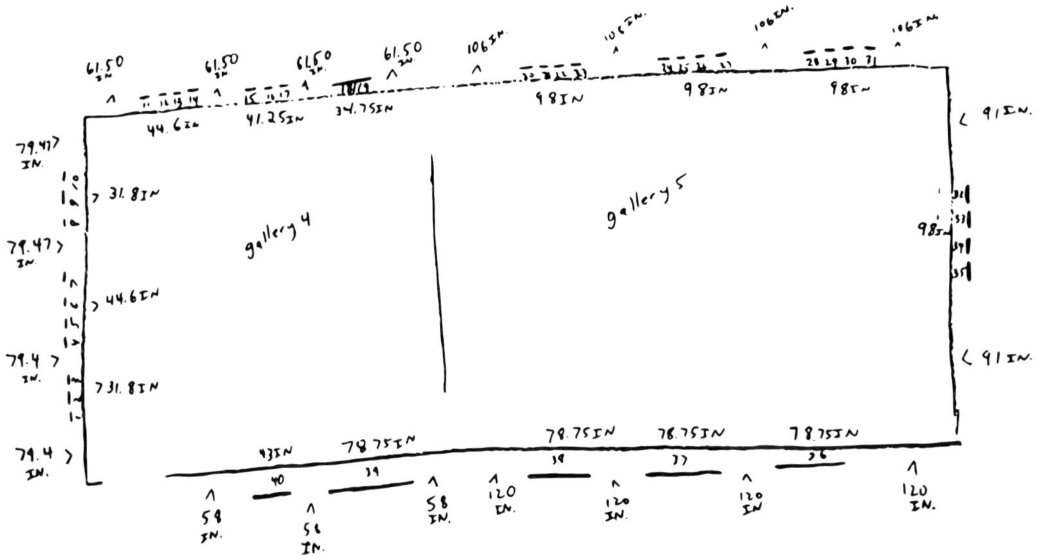

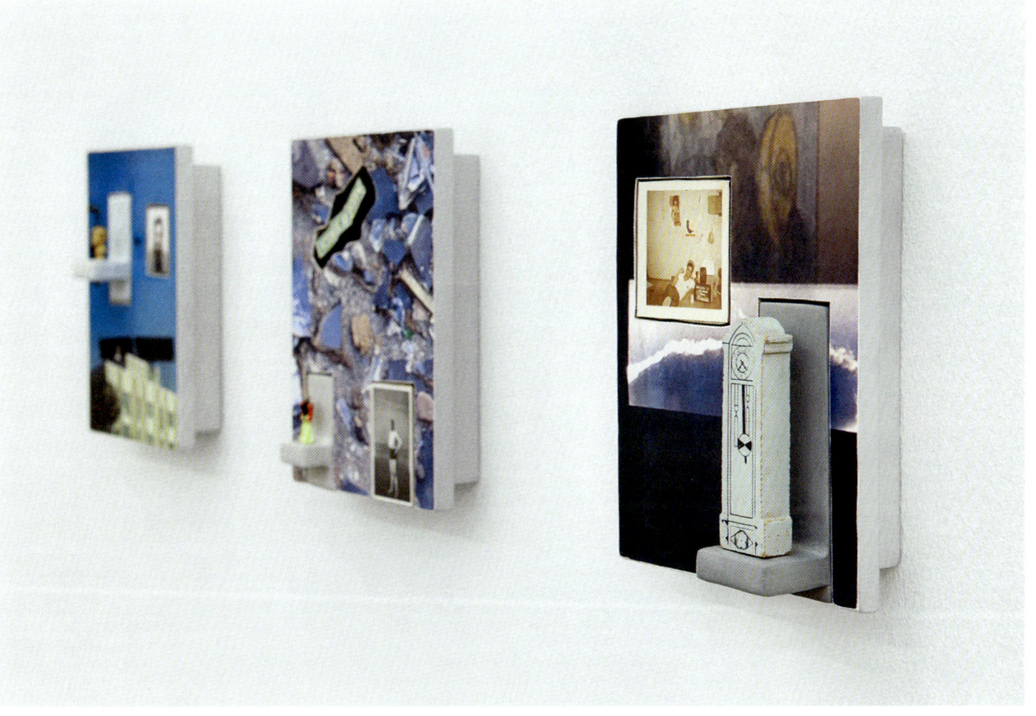

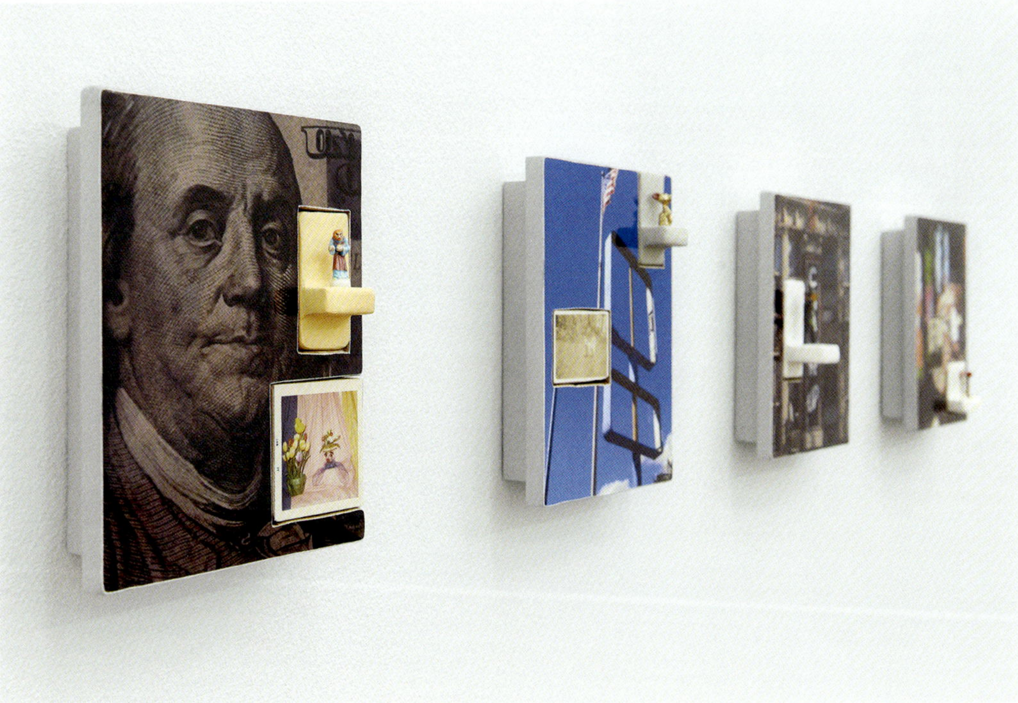

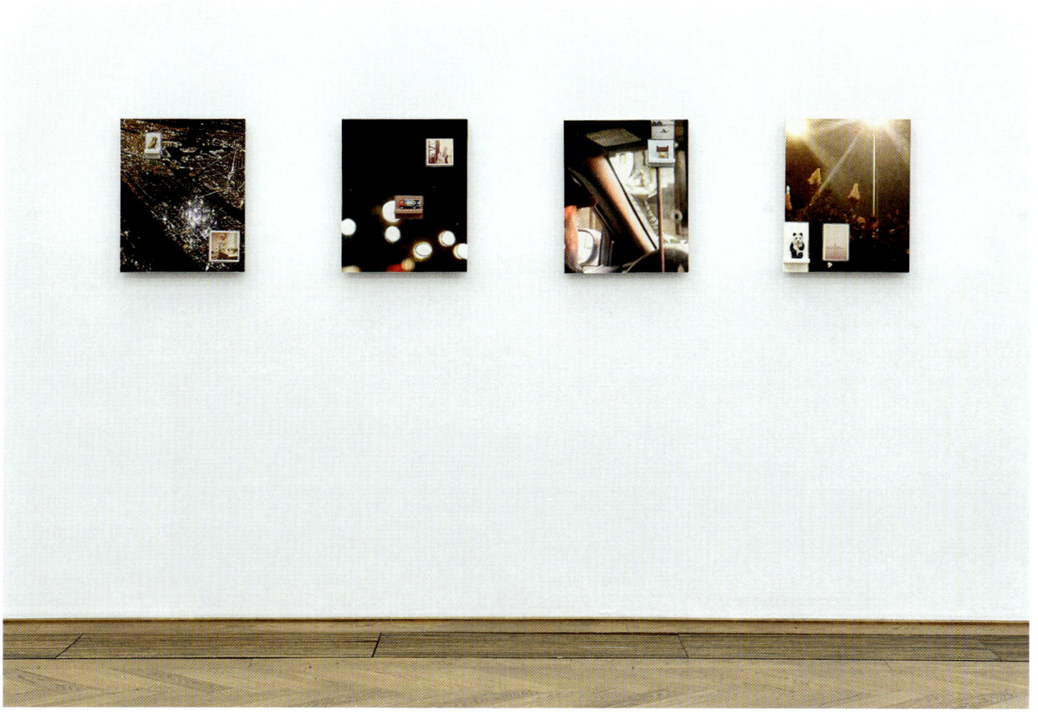

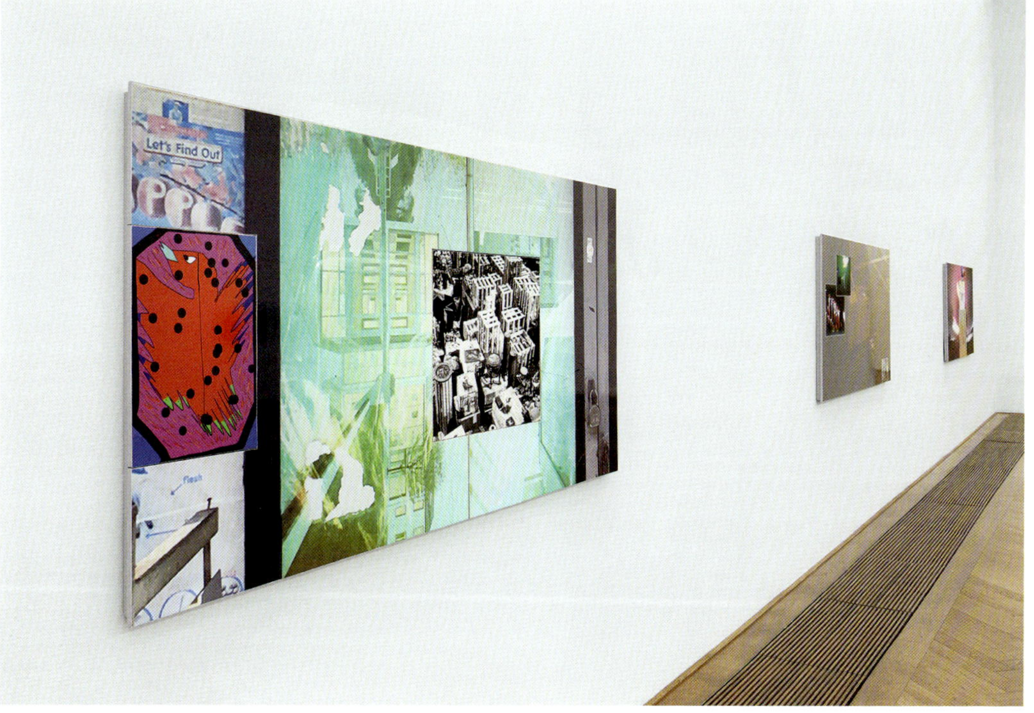
Let's Find Out

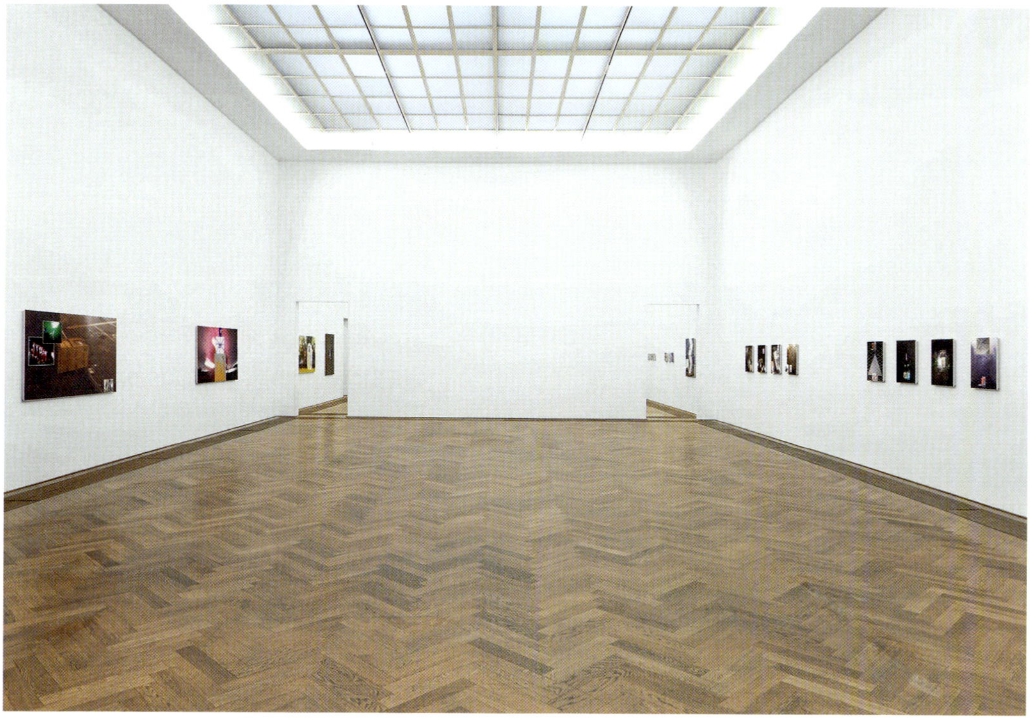

Everybody's Blues

John Corbett

John Corbett

I was in graduate school when Sadie Benning first offered me an eye to share. It was 1990. Benning was 17 and equipped with a Pixelvision camera acquired two years earlier. A teenager already entering the canon of video art with work resonant and premonitory and thunderously original. I think my professor was freaked out that someone so young could make something so powerful as *Jollies*. We sat rapt in silence as Benning posed in front of Prince's "Crazy You," gender fluidity and personal politics brought to the fore with a gentle sense of humor, all braces and Barbie dolls, shot in tender black and white, bordered automatically by the camera within a framing rectangle, a little formal caveat.

Shared Eye, for me, is a film work. A return to film, if we can say that, although I wonder if Benning ever really left. I recall having been pleasantly shocked to see the initial sculptured flatworks at Calicoon Gallery in 2013—paintings, let's call them, though they're more than that—which seemed to approach the body or image but from a hyper-acute angle, stretching or zooming until it becomes nothing but an edge that separates two colors, abstracting it into unrecognizability. Here Benning turned to sculptable aqua resin, which like the children's camera used in the videos, is something readily available, but transformed in the hands of an artist with special vision, an eye that's shared, one that is especially particular and attentive.

A move to and from abstraction, to and from painting, to and from film. Following Blinky Palermo's late work *to the people of N.Y.C.* (1976) as its formal guide, using the German artist's paintings to determine the aspect ratio of and proportional relationships between its parts, Benning's *Shared Eye* orchestrates a sequence of images as an unfolding and developing rhythmic pattern. It consists of a series of edits, occasionally manifesting as formal matches but mostly as jump cuts between photographic image, flat color, and three dimensional object. An overall sense of discontinuity is rolled together into a propositional singularity. Disparateness is resolved, or at least a resolution is proposed, in the form of juxtaposition.

This is not collage or assemblage; it is montage. Montage specifically in Eisenstein's sense: synthesis of symbolic imagery. Except the symbolism here is highly diffuse, differentiated, radial, diverse.

Perhaps one concession to contemporary screen culture is *Shared Eye*'s multifacetedness, the way that its panels nestle thumbnails within larger images as insets, a "scroll montage," but one that's vigorously analog, resisting digitalization. X-acto lines on paper—traces of the process of cutting the image, like scars on the photographs—remind the viewer that this is not a screen, but a physical image, with a skin-like surface. And then there's the nature of the images, found photographs that jostle together as if to tell a story, to turn the film into narrative cinema.

Benning generates a sense of momentum through the progressive increase in size of the panels. There are 40 of them in all, and they are arranged in ascending order as they move clockwise around the room, starting with grouplets of three or four small ones, moving up in scale until the panels are singular and large. And the big ones are just about the same aspect ratio as a common film screen. The grouped panels read as passages or scenes; being grouped together suggests that we read them in relation to one another. So images appear within images and panels alongside panels, and these are all to be seen in the aggregate, as an archive of images, once unrelated and now brought together to make a meaning, a symphonic arrangement. This is Benning's city film, like Walter

Ruttmann's *Berlin: Die Sinfonie der Grosstadt* and Dziga Vertov's *The Man With a Movie Camera*. The city in question in *Shared Eye*, deducing from images of the twin towers and Empire State Building, is the same as Palermo's.

Benning used varying saturations to enhance rhythmic variety and flow. Mostly *Shared Eye*'s images are in color. The '70s Polariods are low-contrast. Some of the black and whites have the golden hue of sepia, others are starker, altogether colorless. There are also vivid contemporary images: the intense oranges, brash reds, and cool blues of the '90s.

Sly little jokes are secret prizes here. A sign saying "Chair Up," next to it a little white shelf with a hobo figurine, as if he's on his own chair up, perhaps at one of the restaurant supply stores on the Bowery. A flagpole with an American flag next to two empty spaces that used to contain store signs, an inset faded image of a pet dog looking like it might occupy one of those blank signs. A golden owl statuette with red eyes and a vase of tulips floating vertiginously over Manhattan at night, shot from a landing plane—clearly the red-eye flying in from somewhere. Some of the contrasting images have a terrible poignancy, a haunting quality. An image of a man holding a rifle, probably an x-mas present, next to him a figurine woman, the relationship left ambiguous, somehow precarious. With the addition of the 3-D objects, the panels function as shrines, Santería outposts, meditation stations on the images they contain. Or is "contain" the wrong word? In fact they don't contain the images. They open them up, set them loose. The panels reveal a deep interconnectedness, adding to a network, the human databank.

The final image is a change-up. From the large single panels, which are horizontal, it changes to vertical. And black. As if a "fin" to the show. But within it is an image of Times Square, which, we can now see, is made up of images, screens, a real-life version of the perpetual insetting in Benning's painting-sculpture-film, and inside of the Times Square shot yet another inset, this time a square Polaroid from some sort of pageant, the king and queen walking away. A bittersweet end to an unspecified reign.

I'm reminded of John Lee Hooker's song "Everybody's Blues." The world puts a hurt on all of us, one time or other. We photograph it and it becomes part of that human databank of joy and suffering. You don't need to know the people or places to understand the feeling. We're all in it together.

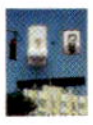
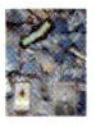
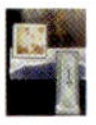

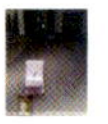
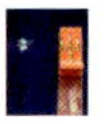
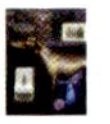
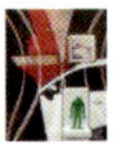
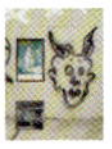
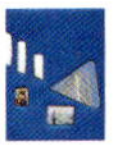
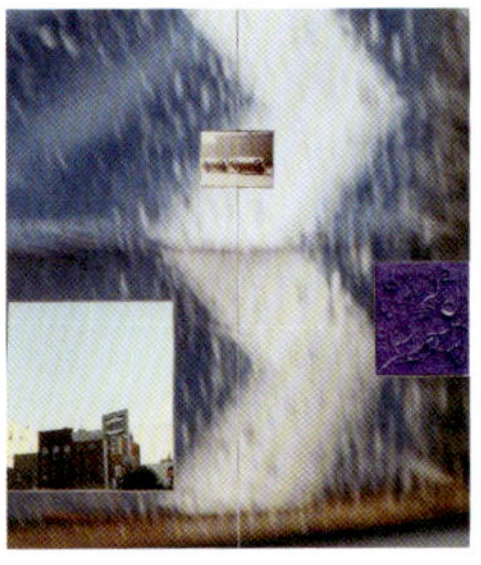
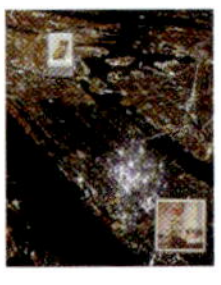
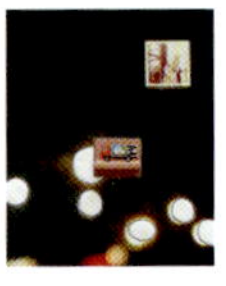
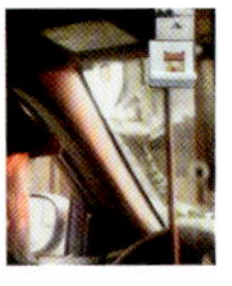
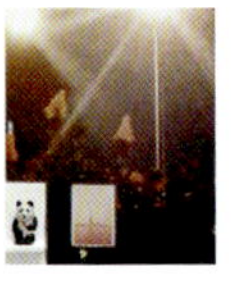
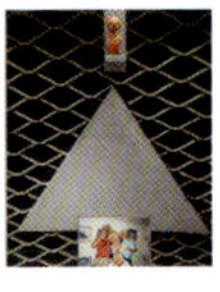
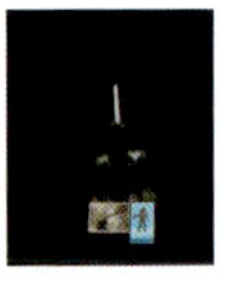
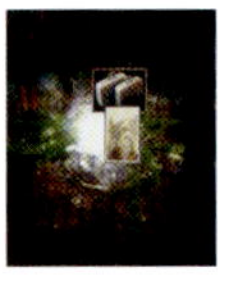
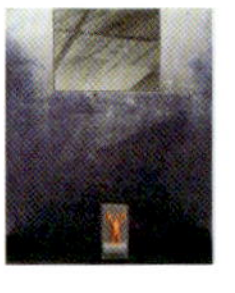
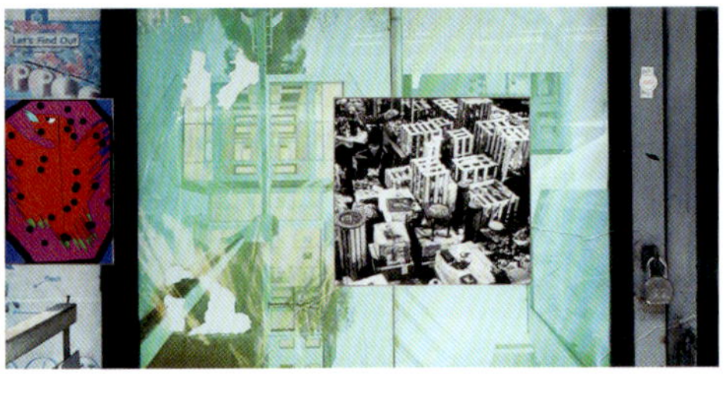
Let's Find Out
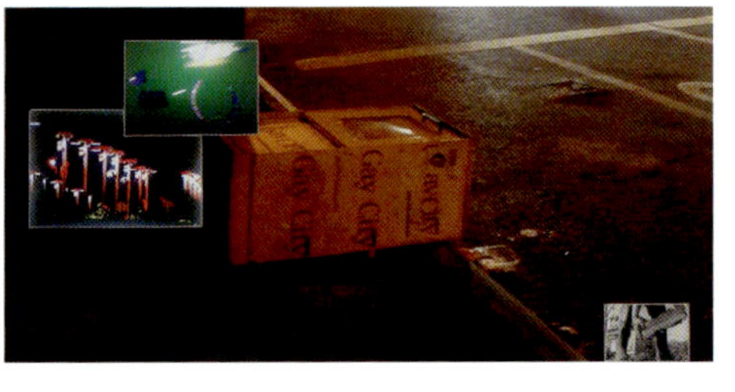
Gay City
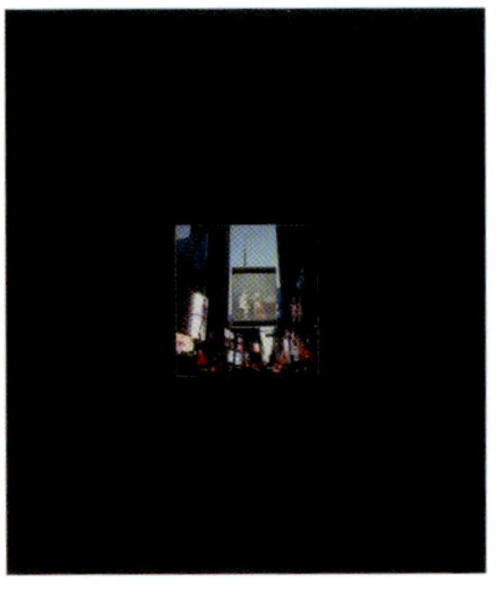

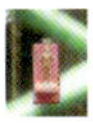
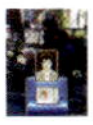
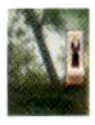
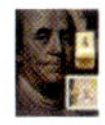
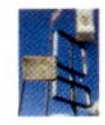
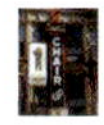
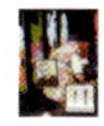
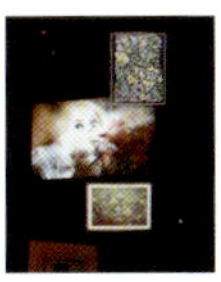
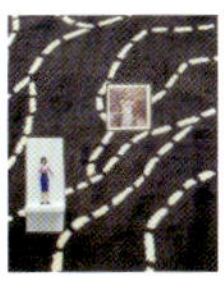
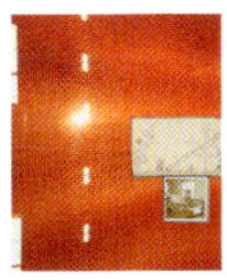
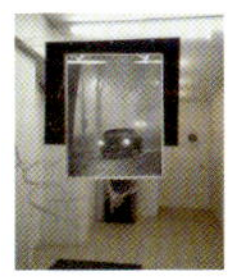
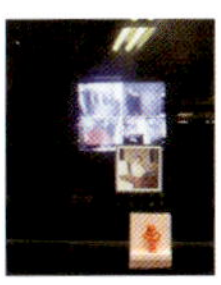
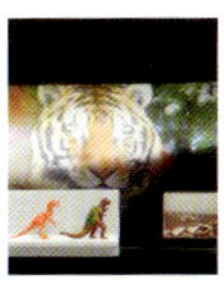
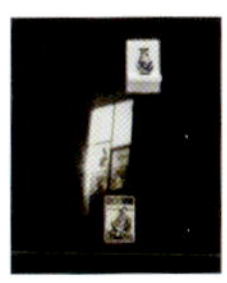
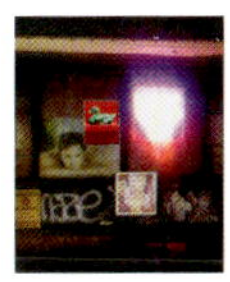
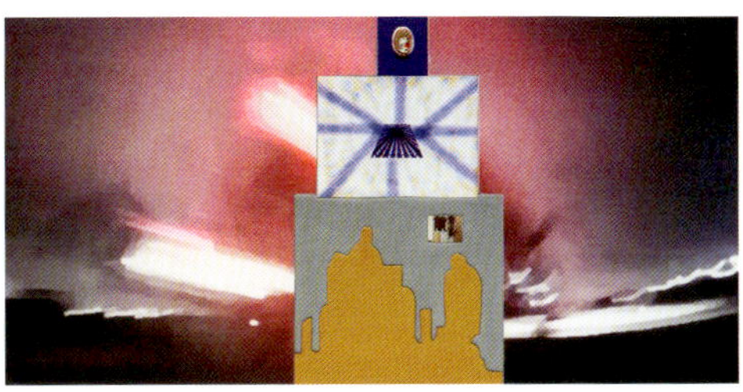
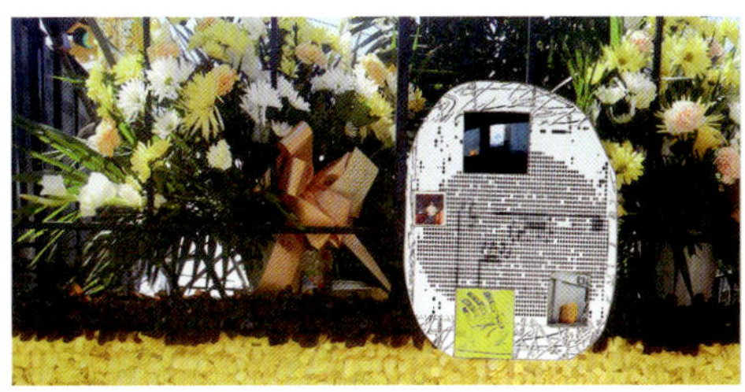

Sadie Benning

BIOGRAPHY

1973 Born in Madison, WI

Lives and works in New York, NY

EDUCATION

1997 MFA, Milton Avery School of Art at Bard College, Annandale-on-Hudson, NY

SELECTED SOLO EXHIBITIONS

2018 *Sleep Rock*, Camden Centre for Arts, London, UK

2017 *Blinded by the Light*, Susanne Vielmetter Los Angeles Projects, Los Angeles, CA

Shared Eye, Kunsthalle Basel, Basel, Switzerland

2016 *Shared Eye*, Renaissance Society, Chicago, IL

Green God, Mary Boone Gallery and Callicoon Fine Arts, New York, NY

L'oeil de l'esprit, Air de Paris, Paris, France

Excuse Me Ma'am, Kaufmann Repetto, Milan, Italy

2015 *Fuzzy Math*, Susanne Vielmetter Los Angeles Projects, Los Angeles, CA

2014 *Patterns*, Callicoon Fine Arts, New York, NY

2013 *War Credits*, Callicoon Fine Arts, New York, NY

2011 *Transitional Effects*, Participant Inc., New York, NY

2009 *Play Pause*, The Whitney Museum of American Art, New York, NY

2008 *Play Pause*, The Power Plant, Toronto, Canada

2007 *Form of... a Waterfall*, Orchard Gallery, New York, NY

Play Pause, Dia Foundation for the Arts, New York, NY

Sadie Benning: Suspended Animation, Wexner Center for the Arts, Columbus, OH

2005 *Sadie Benning's Early Pixelvision Videos*, Walker Art Center, Minneapolis, MN

2004 *Sadie Benning Retrospective Series*, Wexner Center for the Arts, Columbus, OH

SELECTED GROUP EXHIBITIONS

2018 *Photography Today: Private Public Relations*, Pinakothek der Moderne, Munich, Germany

2017 *Trigger: Gender as a Tool and a Weapon*, New Museum, New York, NY

2016 *A Shape That Stands Up*, curated by Jamillah James and organized by Hammer Museum, Art + Practice, Los Angeles, CA

Figurative Geometry, curated by Bob Nickas, Collezione Maramotti, Reggio Emilia, Italy

2015 *Greater NY*, MoMA PS1, New York, NY

Painting 2.0: Expression in the Information Age, Museum Brandhorst, Munich, Germany

2014 *Readykeulous by Ridykeulous: This is What Liberation Feels Like*, Contemporary Art Museum St. Louis, MO

2013 *Macho Man, Tell It To My Heart: Collected by Julie Ault*, Artists Space, New York, NY

2013 Carnegie International, Carnegie Museum of Art, Pittsburgh, PA

NYC 1993: Experimental Jet Set, Trash and No Star, New Museum, New York, NY

2011 *DANCE DRAW*, The Institute of Contemporary Art/Boston, Boston, MA

2010 *OFF Series, Part II*, Center for Contemporary Art, Tel Aviv, Israel

2008 *Annual Report: A Year in Exhibitions*, 7th Gwangju Biennale, South Korea

2004 *Building Identities*, Tate Modern, London, UK

2000 *Whitney Biennial*, Whitney Museum of American Art, New York, NY

MoMA 2000: Open Ends, Modern and Contemporary Art Since 1980, Museum of Modern Art, New York, NY

1999 *Videodrome*, New Museum, New York, NY

1994 *Videotheque: Video Text*, Walker Arts Center, Minneapolis, MN

1993 *Whitney Biennial*, The Whitney Museum of American Art, New York, NY

Venice Biennale, Venice, Italy

1991 *Sadie Benning Videos*, Museum of Modern Art, New York, NY

Hallwalls Contemporary Arts Center, Screening, Buffalo, NY

SELECTED GRANTS AND AWARDS

2005 Guggenheim Fellowship

2003–6 Wexner Center for the Arts, Visiting Artist Residency Award

2000 National Alliance for Media Arts & Culture Merit Award

1999 Andrea Frank Foundation Fellowship

1994 Grande Videokunst Prize, Kahrlsrule, Germany

1993 Film/Video Fellowship, Rockefeller Foundation for the Arts

1993 Midwest Regional Fellowship, National Endowment for the Arts

1992 Los Angeles Film Critics Award, Best Experimental/Independent Film/Video

SELECTED RECENT PUBLICATIONS

2016 *Vitamin P3: New Perspectives in Painting*, Phaidon, London, UK

2013 *2013 Carnegie International*, catalogue, Carnegie Museum of Art, Pittsburgh, PA

2007 *Sadie Benning: Suspended Animation*, catalogue, Wexner Center for the Arts/D.A.P.

SELECTED VIDEO WORK

2013	*War Credits* (16 minute loop, single channel black and white video, sound)
2012	*In Parts* (28min., single channel black and white video, sound)
2011	*Old Waves, Record One* (30min., single channel black and white video)
	Old Waves, Record Two (30min., single channel black and white video)
2006	*Play Pause* (29:21, two channel video installation from hard drive, color digital video/ drawings on paper)
2003	*One Liner* (5:07, installation, black & white video/Pixelvision, sound)
2003	*The Baby* (5:40, installation, color digital video/drawings on paper)
1999	*Aerobicide*, co-director, Kathleen Hanna (5:00, color digital video)
1999	*Le Tigre*, recorded with Kathleen Hanna and Johanna Fateman (vinyl & cd)
1998	*Flat is Beautiful* (56:00, v black & white video/Pixelvision, 16mm, and Super 8)
1995	*German Song* (6:00, black & white video/super 8 film)
1995	*The Judy Spots* (12:30, color video/16 mm film)
1992	*Girl Power* (15:00, black & white video/Pixelvision)
1992	*It Wasn't Love* (19:06, black & white video/Pixelvision)
1991	*A Place Called Lovely* (13:40, black & white video/Pixelvision)
1990	*Jollies* (11:18, black & white video/Pixelvision)
1990	*Welcome to Normal* (20:00, color video/Hi 8)
1990	*If Every Girl Had a Diary* (8:56, black & white video/Pixelvision)
1989	*Living Inside* (5:06, black & white video/Pixelvision)
1989	*Me & Rubyfruit* (5:31, black & white video/Pixelvision)
1989	*A New Year* (5:57, black & white video/Pixelvision)

SELECTED PERMANENT COLLECTIONS

Museum of Contemporary Art, Los Angeles, CA
Art Gallery of Ontario, Toronto, Ontario, Canada
Assocazione Culturale, Bologna, Italy
Beit Berl College, Kfar Saba, Israel
British Film Institute, London, UK
Brown University, Providence, RI
Castello Di Rivoli, Museu D'Arte Contemporanea, Rivoli/Torino, Italy
Center for Arts, Neuchatel, Switzerland
Centre Georges Pompidou, Paris, France
Chungmuro Subway Station, Seoul, Korea
Duke University, Durham, NC

Fondazione Sandretto Re Rebaudengo, Turin, Italy
Fundacio "la Caixa," Barcelona, Spain
Hammer Museum, Los Angeles, CA
Institute of Contemporary Art, Boston, MA
Kansas City Art Institute, Kansas City, MO
Minneapolis Institute of Art, Minneapolis, MN
Museum of Contemporary Art, Chicago, IL
Museum D'art Contemporani, Barcelona, Spain
Museum of Fine Arts, Boston, MA
Museum of Modern Art, New York, NY
Nagoya Multimedia Institution, Nagoyashi, Japan
National Museum of Contemporary Art, Athens, Greece
New York University, New York, NY
Piet Zwart Institute, Rotterdam, The Netherlands
Princeton University, Princeton, NJ
Projects/NRW Forum, Dusseldorf, Germany
RMIT University, Melbourne, Australia
San Francisco Museum of Modern Art, San Francisco, CA
Stanford University, Stanford, CA
Tapies Foundacion, Barcelona, Spain
University of Chicago, Chicago, IL
University of Salamanca, Salamanca, Spain
Walker Art Center, Minneapolis, MN
Whitney Museum of American Art, New York, NY
Yale University, New Haven, CT

Acknowledgements

To realize a pair of exhibitions like *Shared Eye*, as it appeared at our two venues, as well as its accompanying catalogue is, as always, a collective endeavor. Shared indeed, it could not have been completed without the crucial involvement and support of many people. This seems especially fitting for a project concerned with the ways our actions and perceptions might align in various small and large configurations, as individuals and within society.

At the Renaissance Society, we would like to thank the impressive team: Robert Bain, Preparator; Anna Searle Jones, Director of Communications; Maria Lubliner, Director of Finance and Operations; Karsten Lund, Assistant Curator; Julia DeRose, Development Associate; Michael Harrison and Max Guy, both Program and Research Assistants; and Karen Reimer, Publications Director and Registrar. As always, we are grateful to our Board of Directors, and its president Jorge Cauz, for their continuing support.

At Kunsthalle Basel, we extend our gratitude to the entire staff for their dedication, especially to Beatrice Hatebur, General Manager; Renate Wagner, Head of Exhibitions; Klaus Haenisch, Chief Exhibition Technician, with his team, Elena Gerosa, Herbert Rehbein, and Uwe Walther; and Claudio Vogt, Head of Press and Public Programs. We thank as well Franziska Baumgartner and Daniela Brugger, in charge of Educational Services; Rinny Biberstein, Head of Reception and Bookshop, with her team at the reception, including Simone Lappert, Florian Mattmüller, Maximilian Rück, and Lotte Wilhelm; Sören Schmeling, Head of Photo Archive; Regina Vogel, Librarian; Julian Tschudin, Accountant; Gisela Stöckli and Mara Berger, Administration; and Christina Zinsstag, intern.

This publication features new essays by John Corbett and Christine Mehring, which illuminate different aspects of *Shared Eye*, and Julie Ault's wonderful interview with the artist is an equally invaluable resource. We couldn't imagine a better set of perspectives and extend our thanks to all three contributors. We would also like to thank Tom Van Eynde and Philipp Hänger for their installation photographs of *Shared Eye* at the Renaissance Society and Kunsthalle Basel respectively, and David Khan-Giordano for his ever-sterling book design.

Benning's ambitious body of work for these exhibitions was also made possible by the exceptional efforts of Susanne Vielmetter, who provided support and assistance in many ways. We thank her as well as her colleagues at Susanne Vielmetter Los Angeles Projects, including Ariel Pittman. We would also like to extend our great appreciation to Florence Bonnefous, Francesca Kaufmann, Chiara Repetto, and Juan Wauters.

In Chicago the exhibition was generously supported by the Elizabeth Firestone Graham Foundation.

In Basel the exhibition was generously supported by the Volkart Foundation with additional support from the Dr. Georg und Josi Guggenheim-Stiftung. We are grateful for their trust and commitment, as well as to Canton Basel-Stadt and the Basler Kunstverein's Members, Friends, and Commission for their continued and crucial support.

Last, but not least, we extend our deepest gratitude to Sadie Benning, whose generosity and vision shaped ours in our respective venues and indeed shaped this catalogue as a whole.

—Solveig Øvstebø and Elena Filipovic

Photo Credits

pp. 10–87
Sadie Benning, *Shared Eye*, 2016. Casein, acrylic, aqua resin, wood, digital images, photographs, found materials. 40 panels: Panels 1–14: 8 1/4 x 6 3/8 inches (20.9 x 16.21 cm) each; Panels 15–17: 10 1/2 x 8 1/4 in. (26.67 x 20.69 cm) each; Panels 18–19: 39 1/4 x 17 3/8 inches (99.70 x 44.15 cm) each; Panels 20–35: 20 1/2 x 17 inches (52.07 x 43.18 cm) each; Panels 36–39: 39 3/8 x 78 3/4 inches (100.03 x 200.03 cm) each; Panel 40: 49 1/2 x 43 1/4 inches (125.73 x 109.86 cm); © Sadie Benning. Photographs by Chris Austin.

pp. 94, 100, 106, 110, 116
Sadie Benning's studio, New York, 2016. Photographs by Sadie Benning.

pp. 129–137
Installation views, Renaissance Society at the University of Chicago, 2016. Photographs by Tom Van Eynde.

p. 141
Blinky Palermo, *to the people of N.Y.C.*, 1976. Installation view, Dia:Beacon, Beacon, New York, 2003. © Blinky Palermo/Artists Rights Society (ARS), New York. Photograph by Bill Jacobson Studio, New York. Courtesy Dia Art Foundation, New York.

p. 144
Blinky Palermo's studio shortly after his death, Dusseldorf, 1977. Courtesy Palermo Archive, Thordis Moeller, Millertown, New York. Photograph by Imi Knoebel.

Blinky Palermo, Sketch for *to the people of N.Y.C.*, 1976. Acrylic on paper. 9½ x 12¾ inches. Private collection. Courtesy Palermo Archive, Thordis Moeller, Millertown, New York. Photograph by Nic Tenwiggenhorn.

p. 148
Blinky Palermo, *Times of the Day III*, 1975. Private collection. Photo: Bill Jacobson Studio, New York. Courtesy Dia Art Foundation, New York.

p. 151
Josiah McElheny, *Two Grey Disks after a Prototype by Blinky Palermo*, 2011. Two hand-blown, molded glass objects. 8 1/4 x 5 1/4 x 2 1/8 inches. Edition of 30 plus 10 artist proofs. Courtesy of Corbett vs. Dempsey, Chicago, and James Cohan Gallery, New York.

Blinky Palermo, *Untitled*, from the portfolio *4 Prototypen* (4 Prototypes), 1970. One from a portfolio of four screenprints, composition (irreg.): 5 1/4 x 10 7/16" (13.3 x 26.5 cm); sheet: 23 5/8 x 23 5/8" (60 x 60 cm). Publisher: Edition der Galerie Heiner Friedrich, Munich, in cooperation with Edition X, Munich. Printer: Atelier Laube. Edition: 90. Collection Museum of Modern Art, Gift of the Cosmopolitan Arts Foundation. Digital image © The Museum of Modern Art/Licensed by SCALA / Art Resource, NY.

pp. 157–165
Installation views, Kunsthalle Basel, 2017. Photographs by Philipp Hänger/Kunsthalle Basel.

pp. 172–173
Sadie Benning, Mock-up for *Shared Eye*, 2016.

This catalogue is published on
the occasion of the exhibitions
Sadie Benning: Shared Eye

The Renaissance Society
at the University of Chicago
November 19, 2016–January 22, 2017
Curated by Solveig Øvstebø

Kunsthalle Basel
February 10–April 30, 2017
Curated by Elena Filipovic

At the Renaissance Society, the exhibition and catalogue received support from the Elizabeth Firestone Graham Foundation.

At Kunsthalle Basel, the exhibition and catalogue received support from the Volkart Foundation, with additional support by the Dr. Georg und Josi Guggenheim-Stiftung.

Editors: Sadie Benning and Solveig Øvstebø
Publication Director: Karen Reimer
Editorial Assistance: Karsten Lund
Designer: David Khan-Giordano

Printed by EBS Editoriale Bortolazzi Stei, Italy

ISBN: 978-0-941548-70-0